A Very Short, Fairly Interesting and Reasonably Cheap Book About Management

Also in this series:

Chris Grey, *A Very Short, Fairly Interesting and Reasonably Cheap Book About Studying Organizations*

Brad Jackson and Ken Parry, *A Very Short, Fairly Interesting and Reasonably Cheap Book About Studying Leadership*

Jim Blythe, *A Very Short, Fairly Interesting and Reasonably Cheap Book About Studying Marketing*

David Silverman, *A Very Short, Fairly Interesting and Reasonably Cheap Book About Qualitative Research*

George Cairns and Martyna Sliwa, *A Very Short, Fairly Interesting and Reasonably Cheap Book About International Business*

Chris Carter, Stewart Clegg and Martin Kornberger, *A Very Short, Fairly Interesting and Reasonably Cheap Book About Studying Strategy*

Ronnie Lippens, *A Very Short, Fairly Interesting and Reasonably Cheap Book About Studying Criminology*

A Very Short, Fairly Interesting and Reasonably Cheap Book About Management

Ann L. Cunliffe

Los Angeles | London | New Delhi
Singapore | Washington DC

SAGE Publications Ltd
1 Oliver's Yard
55 City Road
London EC1Y 1SP

SAGE Publications Inc.
2455 Teller Road
Thousand Oaks, California 91320

SAGE Publications India Pvt Ltd
B 1/I 1 Mohan Cooperative Industrial Area
Mathura Road
New Delhi 110 044

SAGE Publications Asia-Pacific Pte Ltd
33 Pekin Street #02-01
Far East Square
Singapore 048763

Library of Congress Control Number: 2008943203

British Library Cataloguing in Publication data

A catalogue record for this book is available from
the British Library

ISBN 978-1-4129-3546-3
ISBN 978-1-4129-3547-0 (pbk)

Typeset by C&M Digitals (P) Ltd, Chennai, India
Printed in Great Britain by CPI Anthony Rowe, Chippenham, Wiltshire
Printed on paper from sustainable resources

This book is dedicated to my daughter Lauren,
who also never takes the easy road and who I love dearly.

Contents

About the Author

Ann Cunliffe has recently moved back to the University of New Mexico from Hull University Business School, where she spent two years as Professor of Organization Theory. She is also a Visiting Professor at Leeds and Strathclyde University Business Schools, and has held positions at California State University, and the University of New Hampshire. She is currently the Division Chair of the Critical Management Studies Division at the Academy of Management. Ann's recent publications include *Organization Theory*; collaborating with Mary Jo Hatch on the second edition of *Organization Theory: Modern, Symbolic, and Postmodern Perspectives*; and articles in the *Journal of Management Studies, Organization Studies, Human Relations,* and *Management Learning.* In 2002 she was awarded the 'Breaking the Frame Award' from the *Journal of Management Inquiry,* for the article 'that best exemplifies a challenge to existing thought'. Ann is incoming Editor-in-Chief for *Management Learning,* Associate Editor for *Qualitative Research in Organizations and Management,* and is on the Editorial Boards of *Organization Studies, Human Relations,* the *Scandinavian Journal of Management,* the *Journal of Organizational Change Management,* the *Canadian Journal of Administrative Sciences (CMS),* and the *Employee Responsibilities and Rights Journal.*

She received her Ph.D. and M.Phil. from Lancaster University, UK.

Acknowledgements

Chris Grey came up with the idea of a *Very Short...* book, a readable yet challenging, easily carried book, discussing aspects of organizations not normally covered in textbooks or in the popular press. This different kind of book caught on, and I was fortunate to be given the opportunity to write a *Very Short* book on management. So my first acknowledgements go to Chris for his brainwave and to Kiren Shoman at Sage for trusting me and for her encouragement and perseverance. This became especially important when the book started to take a different path from the original proposal. I've always found that my work seems to write itself, no matter how precise a plan I start with, because I encounter so many thought-provoking ideas that engage me. And once you start thinking about the possibilities those ideas offer ... well, they take you down some interesting paths! So I'm indebted to the people who offered those insights, many of which are embedded somewhere in this book.

I'd especially like to thank colleagues and close friends who have read various chapters, provided constructive feedback, and listened to me with patience: Christine Coupland, Gordon Dehler, Mary Ellen Pratt, Paul Hibbert, Helen Muller, Frank Scott, and John Shotter. To my friends who continue to pave the way, Karen Locke, Jo Hatch, Dvora Yanow, Karen Ashcraft, and Heather Höpfl. And I particularly want to thank John Shotter, who first got me interested in language, and whose inspiration and unfailing support and friendship over the years has kept me going along the paths I'm passionate about. Thank you also to colleagues at Hull University Business School who gave me the much needed support and space to write, and to the anonymous reviewers for their helpful comments on the proposal and draft of the book. Kate Wood and Alan Maloney from Sage have also smoothed the process.

A special mention must go to all the students, who over the years have persevered with many of the ideas in this book, debated them, offered examples of their relevance and of how they've used them in their everyday management practice. Their insights have helped me articulate, refine and situate the notion of relational and reflexive managers – and will continue to do so.

Finally, to my parents for believing in me and for always being there. My Dad is my cheerleader.

Ann
Hull, 2008

Should You Buy this Book?

Who is it for?

- Students of management and business studies interested in a career in management who want to understand management from different perspectives.
- Postgraduate students of management and business studies who have some experience and realize that managing is not as easy as most textbooks make out.
- Managers who want to read something that's both intellectually challenging and useful.
- Academics who are interested in less conventional ideas about management and who want ideas for challenging conversations with students.

Why buy it?

- You think there's something more to management than 5 Steps, SWOTs, Maslow, LMX, and lists of principles.
- You want to read something different about management and what managers do.
- You are fed up with all those self-assessment questionnaires designed to make you a better manager.
- You work for someone who has an MBA and always does great on all those self-assessment questionnaires – yet still manages to irritate the heck out of everyone at work.
- You want to think more critically about management and managing.
- You like challenges.
- You are about to get on a seven-hour flight to goodness knows where, you've forgotten your iPod, and your only other options are romantic novels or autobiographies of people you've never heard of.

And if you do buy it and want to discuss anything, please email me at cunliffe@mgt.unm.edu.

Introduction

After we emerged,
The world was flat and life
was too easy.
We soon forgot about our makers.
So they created the mountains, mesas and valleys
to make us humble
and make us repentant.
This is what our fathers tell us.

Isleta Pueblo, Theodore Jojola

I was wandering through the Indian Pueblo Cultural Center in Albuquerque, when I came across this story of emergence – the birth of the Native American people from the earth. As one of the oldest cultures in the USA, the Pueblo Indians have a rich and fascinating history, but one that is also a story of oppression, initially by the Spanish and then by the US Federal Government. It's a culture of survival and of difference. One of the most spectacular sites in New Mexico is that of the Acoma Pueblo, which sits on a 370-feet-high sheer mesa nearly 6,500 feet above sea level. Acoma is an oral and a matriarchal society, with property being passed down to the youngest daughter in the family. When the Catholic Mission was built in the mid-1600s, under Spanish direction, Native American traditions and symbols were incorporated seemingly surreptitiously into the building – a form of symbolic resistance?[1] You cannot fail to connect with the different way of living at Acoma, adapted and preserved throughout the experience of being colonized.

Why do I begin with this story? Because when I first read it, it struck me that it offered a metaphor for the history and development of Management Studies: that most management theorizing over the last century focused on smoothing out the landscape into nice cultivatable and manageable chunks. It wasn't until the advent of Critical Management Studies that the complexities of the landscape became visible and caused us to question the orderly management world we'd constructed and colonized. There are also connections between the story and this book. Yes, it's a 'short' book, but not one about a flat world, about making management simple and managing easier – a world that's been colonized by seemingly rational techniques. It is about the mountains, mesas and valleys, the hidden aspects of the management landscape, which might come into view when we start poking and prodding around into issues such as the nature of language, organizational 'reality', and the implications for managing organizations and people. And, given the influential role of managers and organizations in the world today, the book is also about humility in the sense of recognizing our ethical and moral responsibility, as managers and academics, to others.

This book is written about management and for managers and students of management, rather than academics. It's about questioning who managers are and what they do, and is written with Chris Grey's original purpose in mind, that it be a different kind of book with, I hope, thought-provoking ideas and ways of thinking about, doing and being a manager. Most management books normally cover topics such as finance, marketing, operations management, motivation, teamwork, project management, performance management, etc. To write yet another book addressing such topics seems to me to defeat the purpose of the *Very Short...* series, because writing about 'business as usual' or 'management in five minutes' tells us nothing new. Nor does it cause us to consider alternative views and perspectives. In writing a more critical book on management, the crucial question seems to me to be: *In a landscape of sameness, what features strike us as being worth exploring because they encourage us to see things differently?* We are going to examine aspects of management that are often taken for granted and treated as add-ons by other management books, yet which I believe are embedded within everyday management practice and integral to the effective management of people and organizations – communication, encountering difference, and acting ethically.

Let's begin with the common definition of management as 'getting things done and achieving organizational goals through people'. We will look at the various ways in which authors have prescribed how this should occur ... and explore a different perspective. A perspective that suggests whether you are a CEO, a production, finance or marketing manager, that *managing is a relational practice*. In other words, managing is embedded in relationships with people, in what we say and do, and therefore we need to understand the crucial nature of language and our everyday communicative practices. This is why there's a chapter on language in a book on management.

The journey takes us along a path that requires us to address some basic issues that philosophers have been struggling with for many years. We'll draw on the work of scholars such as Ferdinand de Saussure, Paul Ricoeur, Maurice Merleau-Ponty, Mikhail Bakhtin, Judith Butler and Joan Acker, linguists, philosophers and feminists who are concerned about the relationship of language, our world and ourselves. But before you yawn, close the book and put it back on the shelf, let me say that we'll discuss these issues from a very practical perspective, with the question of how they relate to managing organizations at the forefront. I am not a philosopher, but there are aspects of philosophy that fascinate me, particularly phenomenological, existential, hermeneutic and poststructuralist work which grapples with questions such as:

- What is the nature of social reality?
- Who are we?
- What does it mean to be an ethical person and act in moral ways?

These questions are interesting – not just from an intellectual perspective, but from a practical one – because they play into how we see ourselves and others, and how we live our lives with other people on an everyday and ongoing basis. They are also fundamental to managing organizations. Our beliefs about what managers should be doing are based on a primary set of assumptions about the way the world operates. But a good deal of management theorizing takes these assumptions for granted, and does not accept there are any alternative versions. In other words, the world is flat, uniform, unidimensional – and life is relatively easy. Management education also for the most part operates within this context, and is part of the process of socializing people into becoming 'good' managers and 'good' organizational citizens – with a particular view of the world and definition of 'good' in mind.

Take, for example, the assumption underlying much of management theory today – that individuals are self-actualizing, operating in a social world that exists independently from them – versus the assumption that we are always in relation to other people and that we are continually shaping our social world in our everyday interactions. How might these assumptions affect how I view myself as a manager, how I do my job, and the way I interact with employees? How might they influence what I see as 'good' knowledge? These are the issues and questions we'll discuss throughout the book.

I can't claim that understanding management from a philosophical perspective is a new idea. Indeed, going back to a 1960 *Harvard Business Review* article, 'Existentialism for the businessman', John Rice stated, 'All businessmen, whether or not we admit it, are philosophers in a sense. Philosophy provides a framework within which we interpret our experiences and judge ourselves and situations' (1960: 135). What struck me about this article was first that its author was a business person who presumably had taken the time to read some philosophy and write about it at a time when it was not 'cool' to do so, and second that it was published in *Harvard Business Review* – a journal not noted for publishing philosophical articles, rather as a bastion of managerialism! So what happened to management in the intervening 40 years? The advent of Critical Management Studies in the 1980s and 1990s brought philosophy and critique to European management schools, but these ideas are still on the fringe of North American business schools.

So bear with me, and persevere with the ideas in the book. They are about encountering difference and they are, I believe, crucially important to managers. You'll notice a number of paths through the landscape that at some points separate and others converge, but that always head in the same general direction – that how we relate to people and the world around us is the core of every aspect of management. The first path explores the relationship between language and our experience of the world, a relationship we often take for granted, and moves on to examine the impact that assumptions of socially constructed realities have on management theory and practice. The second is about encountering difference, the gendered nature of organizations and management, and how managers deal with gendered notions of identity and organizing. The third is about ethics – not the normal path of business ethics which focuses on codes of conduct, but how to *be* ethical in our relationships and interactions with others.

As you'll see, at the heart of the book is a fundamental questioning of who we are (as people and as managers) and how we experience organizational life and relate to other people. You may or may not agree with the ideas in the book – given my beliefs it would be hypocritical and unreflexive of me to say my way of viewing the world is the 'right' one. But it's the thinking through of these ideas, examining their practicality, assessing their possibilities, and figuring out where you stand that's important. And I've been encouraged over the years by the response of students, which often turns from cynicism, to interest, to engagement. You'll find comments from my conversations with managers and students throughout the book, to illustrate the ways in which they have connected the issues with their own experience as managers.

As German philosopher Martin Heidegger argues in *Discourse on Thinking* (1966), truth is not about finding *the* one reality or right way, but is concerned with understanding the grounds of our thinking – and to do so we need to empty ourselves of accepted ways of thinking and open ourselves to other possibilities. To do so we need to question taken-for-granted rules and practices, the questions we ask, and the answers we seek. He has a really neat way of explaining this different way of thinking, by differentiating between calculative thinking and meditative thinking. I would like to illustrate this by borrowing from his conversation between a Scientist, a Scholar and a Teacher:

Conversation on the Way to Class (with apologies to Heidegger)

STUDENT A: So, have you finished our required readings for this course, the *Very Short...* and the piece from *Discourse on Thinking*?

STUDENT B: Yes, it was challenging to say the least! I'm still trying to work out how Saussure's and Heidegger's ideas relate to managing an organization.

STUDENT A: Well, this book is certainly different from our other management textbooks, which at least are clear about how to handle the problems we face. Yet there are some ideas that at the moment I can't quite grasp, but might be interesting if I could figure out what they meant. This whole idea that there's no reality independent from language, that managers are story tellers ... And Heidegger's terminology is confusing. Why does he write in the form of a conversation between three people? He could convey his ideas more clearly if he just wrote them in a straightforward way ...

STUDENT B: ... like a factual report with an executive summary, rather than a fictional conversation – he's probably seen our monthly ops reports, which tend to be more fictional than factual! *[laughter]* Maybe it's linked to his distinction between calculative and meditative thinking? My understanding is that calculative thinking is typical of modern scientific knowledge; making sense of what's going on around us, figuring out what's happening and why, understanding what things mean so we can plan and organize. I think that's why he talks about calculative thinking as *willing*, that we *will* something into being, or we make it happen by thinking about it as real.

STUDENT A: Hmmm... I think *it* therefore *it* exists – the process of representation. I think it's the Scientist who states that scientific methodology is grounded in 'the relation of man as ego to the thing as object'. As a 'scientific' manager I can define, categorize and manipulate things – surely that's what we need to do to get the job done? We're on this management course to learn how to create organization structures, strategies and systems so we can get things done more efficiently and effectively. We need calculative thinking to *will* those into being.

STUDENT B: Yes ... but what if those 'things' depend on us, on our ways of talking and 'seeing'? You know, we often say, 'You just don't get it, if only you could see it my way!'

STUDENT A: Seeing another way ... doesn't that involve what Heidegger calls meditative thinking ... thinking imaginatively, with other possibilities in mind?

STUDENT B: Yes ... I think so ... it's quite different from calculative thinking ...

STUDENT A: ... Meditative thinking means opening ourselves up to hidden meanings and possibilities ...

STUDENT B: Yes. I think Heidegger is saying that because calculative thinking focuses on representing a reality, it encloses and fixes truths – and by doing so, we then just accept things the way we *think* they are. How many times do we say at work 'Oh we can't change that, it's the system' – as though the system has a life of its own? Meditative thinking involves waiting for the *mystery* – whatever strikes us or withdraws from us at any moment. So instead of willing things into truth, we move away from what we often take for granted and see as being obvious – like *the system* – and open ourselves to hidden meanings ...

STUDENT A: ... so instead of trying to discover the *real* reality and truth, we think about the assumptions underlying our ways of thinking and acting and become more open to possibilities ... Isn't that what managing reflexively is? Look here, where the Scientist says: 'As I see more clearly, all during our conversation I have been waiting for the arrival of the nature of thinking. But waiting itself has become clearer to me now ...' Well, this way of thinking doesn't make life any simpler does it?!

STUDENT B: No! But as Heidegger says, we should be 'Apparently emptier, but richer in contingencies'!

And this is what the book is about – the *mystery* and some of the hidden features of managing.

      note

I   See http://sccc.acomaskycity.org/visiting.

1

Management, Managerialism and Managers

When I was asked to write this book, there was some debate about the title: should it be about management, managers or managing people? Why was this an issue? We often use the terms interchangeably without necessarily thinking about the implications or consequences. But I believe language is important. This is not just a semantic or an intellectual issue, it's also a practical one, because whether we are aware of it or not, words do things – they influence and play out in our actions and relationships. Consider how a person's actions and ways of speaking and relating to other organizational members change in overt and subtle ways when she or he becomes a 'manager' and part of a management team. So it's worth spending some time exploring these differences and examining their potential practical consequences. The purpose of this chapter is to examine the often taken-for-granted and generally narrow ways in which we think about management, and to offer some alternative ways of thinking about what managers do and who managers are. We'll touch on the relationship between management and language in this chapter, but go on to explore this in more depth in Chapter 2.

To begin with some brief definitions: *management* is a collective noun used to refer to a group of people engaged in organizing and controlling a business or, as Tony Watson and Pauline Harris (1999) say, management is a requirement and outcome of any work organization. We also talk about Management Studies as a body of knowledge, skills and competencies associated with managing organizations. *Managers* are people who engage in these activities, and *managing* relates to the activity of doing something to and/or with others. In the first *Very*

Short... book, Chris Grey (2008: 55–63) talks about the origins and interpretations of management: from the mundane meaning of managing to do something (I *managed* to get out of bed today), to the elitist view of management as a dominant social institution and an instrument of control. He outlines what it is that managers do when they manage: they solve problems, they control and discipline workers, they make things efficient, they might even make things more humane. They do so by representing and intervening: making activities and actions knowable by producing signs and texts (organization charts, job descriptions, product specifications, operational procedures, etc.), and then acting to make sure people and things do what they are supposed to be doing.

Much of the literature on management, both traditional and contemporary, focuses on answering the questions 'What *is* management?' and 'What do/should managers *do*?' Even critical perspectives (CMS) address these questions, although their answers might be very different from the norm. These questions are seen as vital to the development of 'professional' managers because management education and training programmes are based on theories, models and ideas about the types of activities carried out by effective managers. If education can equip managers with the knowledge, techniques and skills necessary for them to function more effectively, then an improvement should be seen in organizational and ultimately economic performance. However, there's a performative element to management that often remains unconsidered. *Performativity* draws on the notion that words are not just words, they *do* things. John L. Austin (1962) argued that we create action when we utter particular kinds of words. For example, 'You are fired' or 'You are now promoted to Human Resource Director', has an influence on how a person behaves – in the latter example on ways we expect HR Directors to behave and talk. Feminist philosopher Judith Butler has done much to develop the notion of performativity, particularly in relation to gender-identity. Let's look at some of her ideas because they pave the way for looking at performativity in a management context. In *Gender Trouble*, first published in 1990, Butler draws on Austin's notion that words do things to argue controversially that gender is *performative*. Gender and identity do not exist *per se*, but are ongoing and open, created, maintained and refashioned in our desires, words, gestures, acts and social discourse. We might have the illusion of a given and stable gender-identity, but it is an effect, a 'repeated stylization of the body, a set of repeated acts within a highly rigid regulatory frame that congeal over time to produce the appearance of substance, of a natural sort of being' (1990: 43–4). So for Butler, gender and identity are performed and come into being through language, are neither fixed nor free-floating but 'performatively constituted by the very "expressions" that are said to be its results' (p. 33).

If we relate this to managerial identity, then the very words 'managers', 'management', and 'managing' and all that they convey (as we will see in the discussion to follow), construct the very behaviours and actions they supposedly describe. There is an extensive body of scholarship relating to management that carries the assumption that theory informs practice, and that good managers need to be able to talk the talk *and* walk the talk. This work includes articles, books, management degree programmes and training activities, which have created and maintained management as we know and enact it today. Embedded in this work are ways of talking about and framing management that are authoritative forms of speech, bringing ways of acting and forms of managerial identity into being. For example, the term 'management by walking about' (MbWA) was popularized by Tom Peters and Robert Waterman in their 1982 book *In Search of Excellence*, and is now an accepted part of management discourse and practice. So words both *author* managerial action and identity, and give that action and identity *authority* and power over others – an example of performativity.

There is little doubt that management theory has played an influential role in management education by providing both the language and the organizing themes for curriculum design, guidelines for course content and topics for teaching. Yet despite this, the relationship between management theory and practice is seen to be problematic. The assumption that theory informs practice came under scrutiny over twenty years ago with criticisms that theory is divorced from practice and doesn't take into account the complexities and uncertainties managers face.[1] The debate still continues today. A number of authors have attempted to bridge the gap. Tony Watson's ethnography of how managers work in a UK company, documented in *In Search of Management* (1994, revised 2001) is one such example. Another quite different attempt is *Thinking About Management* (2000), where Ian Palmer and Cynthia Hardy aim to link academic management debates to practical management issues by organizing the debates around management activities such as: managing structure, managing people and managing power. While Watson's account is an inductive one, based on insights drawn from his conversations with managers during a year spent in a company, Palmer and Hardy's book is deductive, still essentially theoretical with practical management-related exercises. In the main, management theory is still 'theoretical'.

Just as Judith Butler argues that we need to challenge ways of thinking about gender and identity to reveal their political nature and ontological possibilities, so have there been calls to critically interrogate taken-for-granted approaches to management, managing, and management education.[2] We'll take up the challenge in this and the following chapters. In this chapter, we'll look at the various – and often unproblematic – ways in which management and managers have been constructed, both in the literature and in practice. We'll do so as a way of establishing the groundwork for one of the major premises of this book, that:

> Management is not just something one *does*, but is more crucially, *who one is and how we relate to others.*

In order to examine this statement more carefully, we'll move on to explore different ways of thinking about management and managing. Our 'realities', identities, and even knowledge itself, are culturally, historically and linguistically situated, so we'll begin with an overview of how Management Studies has developed over the last century. When reading this, you might notice that the history of management is western (based mainly in the USA and Europe), and it's a history mainly by men, about men, and for men. This may seem to be a controversial statement, but when I started teaching in a UK Business School over 25 years ago, there were only two female management faculty members and we often taught management courses with no female students. Before the 1970s, there were few female management or organization theory authors (Mary Parker Follett, Rosabeth Kanter and Rosemary Stewart being exceptions). So management was, and as we will see in Chapter 3, largely still is *man*agement, not just in terms of the number of male versus female managers, but also in relation to the gendered nature of organizational practice.

I also want to suggest that despite the debate about whether management theory has any relevance to management practice, there are connections. Those connections occur because managers and aspiring managers read books about management, study for management degrees and attend management training courses, all of which include management theory and techniques. Academics research and consult in organizations, and their findings form part of business school curricula. So management discourse and practice are interwoven to an extent. Management is performative, and we will see the nature of this performativity in the discussion that follows. I also want to suggest that it's this process that we need to interrogate critically.

management and managerialism

The emergence of management in this [twentieth] century may have been a pivotal event of history. It signaled a major transformation of society into a pluralist society of institutions, of which managements are the effective organs.

Peter F. Drucker, 1973: 1

To recap, *management* can be seen variously as a group of people managing an organization, a body of knowledge and competencies, a social form, and a practice. Firstly, we talk about *management* as a group of people differentiated from other groups – professional, technical, scientific, manual and administrative employees. This differentiation occurs in linguistic and symbolic ways that play out in everyday interactions and conversations. Linguistically, written documents such as job descriptions, policy and procedure manuals outline the particular responsibilities and rights of management, and we talk about white-collar (management and professional) and blue-collar (non-management and professional) employees. Symbolically, management is often differentiated by dress, physical space and office decor, the type of technology, equipment and 'tools' used, parking spaces, and so on. Practically, those in management are often salaried employees who receive rewards and fringe benefits that other employees do not. Management is also seen as a social form and practice: a recognizable career with responsibilities, rights and privileges considered legitimate not only by organizational members, but also by members of society. Being 'a manager' carries a certain status within society. And as Peter Drucker states in the quote at the beginning of this section, management is the organ or instrument enabling an institution to function, by ensuring the institution achieves its mission; making work and workers productive; and by 'managing social impacts and social responsibilities' (1973: 40). And management does so by producing economic results.

But how did management become so central to modern society? Figure 1 offers one way of making sense of how management has developed as a topic of study and practice over the last century. I have identified four distinct but overlapping phases, associated with developments in management research, theory and practice. The 'Academic Lens' axis relates to the major schools of thought – recognized ways of studying management and organizations. Each phase highlights a particular interest and approach to management research and practice. Figure 1 captures Bakhtin's (1986) notion of speech genres (see Chapter 2) because it draws together a number of secondary speech genres – the organized, ideological and theoretical forms of talk that combine to form the Discourse of Management Studies.

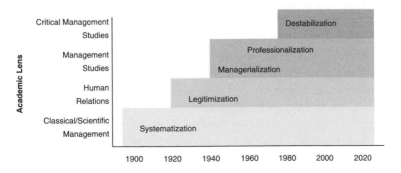

Figure 1   A brief history of management

in the beginning: systematization...

In the early twentieth century, management and organization studies did not exist as a formal discipline or practice. There was no recognizable body of knowledge or profession known as management. A number of academics and practitioners began a search for the best way of managing and designing organizations, which they believed could be achieved by developing more 'scientific' and systematic approaches to managing organizations. Their work is collectively known as the Classical and Scientific Management Schools of thought, which formed the prehistory of management studies and played a major role in the systematization, legitimization and professionalization of the field. The impact of Classical and Scientific Management is still felt today in Business School curricula and in management practice. Because this book is about management rather than organization studies in general, I'm going to focus on a few key figures in the field of Management Studies.[3]

We can begin the story of the systematization and legitimization of management with Frederick Taylor's book *The Principles of Scientific Management* (1911). Taylor, Chief Engineer at the Bethlehem Steel Company in Philadelphia, was concerned with developing a more systematic approach to management through the identification and application of scientific principles that would simultaneously allow the maximization of profit and wage-earning capability through the lowering of production costs and by increasing employee efficiency. He set out a number of principles he saw as necessary for efficient management, including the scientific analysis of work and the systematic hiring and training of employees. Taylor's work became the basis for time and motion studies and helped legitimize management as a profession and a social form by establishing a set of 'scientific' management practices. Yet his work was not without its critics, most notably in relation to the deskilling and dehumanization of the work environment. One need only watch the first ten minutes of Charlie Chaplin's satirical 1936 film *Modern Times*, notably the automated feeding machine designed to feed workers while they worked, to grasp the effect of the Taylor system on the well-being and the morale of employees. The film also highlights Fordism, a system of production named after Henry Ford, who adopted scientific management principles in his auto manufacturing business in the 1920s. Fordism incorporates the mass production of goods through an assembly line process in which work is broken down into unskilled, standardized and highly repetitive tasks.

● ... along with legitimization...

In addition to Taylor, Mary Parker Follett, Henri Fayol, Luther Gulick and Chester Barnard also wrote influential books on management. Mary Parker Follett was a pioneering American scholar and management consultant who examined the nature of power, advocated individual and community development, and democratic forms of organization, including self-governing groups, as long ago as 1918. Her radical (for the time) interest in social consciousness, participative decision-making, and in developing community-based rather than hierarchical structures, was echoed later by Chester Barnard, President of the New Jersey Bell Telephone Company. In his 1938 book *The Functions of the Executive*, Barnard argued that managers needed to create cooperative organizational systems in which work should be integrated by establishing and communicating goals and motivating workers to achieve the goals. Contrast Follett's ideas with those of Fayol, CEO of a French mining company, whose work is explicitly and implicitly concerned with establishing the right of managers to manage. In his 1916 book *General and Industrial Management*, Fayol specified five functions of management (planning, organizing, commanding, coordinating and controlling), along with 14 principles of administration, which included the unity-of-command (each subordinate reporting only to one boss) and the scalar principle, where all organizational members are to be controlled by being placed in a hierarchical structure resembling a pyramid. Gulick, a Professor of Municipal Science and Administration at Columbia University in the 1930s, built on Fayol's work by devising the famous mnemonic (POSDCoRB) to describe the functions of a chief executive: Planning, Organizing, Staffing, Directing, Coordinating, Reporting and Budgeting. Gulick's work had a major impact on the management of public sector and government organizations, primarily in the USA, but also in the UK. It's interesting to note that while Taylor's, Fayol's, Barnard's and Gulick's work essentially accepted and reinforced a manager's right to manage, Follett's (1924) ground-breaking work emphasized what she called *power-with* rather than power-over: the joint development of power based on interactive influence between community members and between organizational members. She argued that the development of power-with takes time, but is important because this form of power is a true reflection of the democratic ideals of society.

The Human Relations School, which began with the Hawthorne Studies in the 1920s, shifted the focus to the need for managers to consider people and the social factors at play in work. While the studies began by examining the impact of the work environment on productivity, the researchers discovered that issues such as consultation, informal group processes, and the motivation of workers were influential factors in worker productivity. While the Hawthorne Studies are criticized in terms of their experimental validity, they nevertheless offered an important turning point in management and are regarded as the foundation of Organizational Behaviour because they led to studies of individual and group behaviour, motivation, leadership and communications. It is also worth noting that while this concern for people and the humanization of management is ostensibly altruistic, at its heart lies a concern for improving productivity by controlling the behaviour of employees.

If we go back to Chris Grey's idea that management is a process of representation and intervention, then we can see this occurring in these two phases of management. Systematization is about trying to make management knowable by naming and re-presenting activities, behaviours and responsibilities, and by establishing a bag of management tools that can be used to manage organizations efficiently and effectively. By creating this formal body of expertise based on 'scientific' principles and activities, management becomes more credible and managers more authoritative because they have legitimate intervention techniques to control people, direct their activities and make changes. I suggest systematization and legitimization are also about difference and distance. By creating specialized knowledge, management becomes different and separate from other professions, jobs and work activities. And difference and distance are seen as essential to maintaining control – as Taylor argued, managers should manage and workers do the work.

● managerialization and managerialism...

Managerialism is often associated with the rise of the managerial class and of a managerialist ideology. Peter Drucker (1973) saw the period between the Second World War and the 1960s as a management boom that changed society permanently because management became a familiar term, a legitimate social practice, and a position of status supported by institutional and social norms that gave managers the right to hire, fire, give orders, control and evaluate the performance of others in the interest of efficiency, productivity, profit or providing a service for the common good.[4] Chris Grey suggests that consequently management became the 'bulwark of civilization', yet also ironically a 'perennially failing operation' because organizational and managerial problems continue to demand new and improved techniques and approaches. This failure has led to the growth of Human Resource Management, Management and Organization Studies, management consultants, and the emergence of management gurus such as W. Edwards Deming and Tom Peters.

Along with the management boom came managerialism which, as Stan Deetz argues in *Democracy in an Age of Corporate Colonization*, is 'a kind of systemic logic, a set of routine practices, and an ideology ... a way of doing and being' in organizations which has the ultimate goal of enhancing efficiency through control (1992: 222). But what does this mean, and how does ideology relate to management practice?

An *ideology* is a system of beliefs, values, ideas, interests, social structures and practices that explicitly and implicitly shape the way we see and make sense of our experience. This system inevitably has an underlying logic that also influences the way we do things, and that we use to evaluate what is good or bad, appropriate or inappropriate action. Capitalism is a prime example – the belief that organizations have to be managed for the economic benefit of owners. The American Dream and the Protestant Work Ethic are also examples of ideologies that play through our organizational lives in formal (such as through promotion criteria and personal development activities) and informal (everyday action) ways. The American Dream, the belief that we can gain material wealth, success, happiness and be who we want to be if we work hard and strive to achieve, has practical consequences for the ways in which US organizations are managed and employees are evaluated and promoted. Organization cultures often value individualism, competitiveness, risk taking, assertiveness and 'doing what it takes' to get short-term results: values that Geert Hofstede (1985, 2001) found to be typically American. In his study of the IBM Corporation in different countries, he found each country held different cultural values, for example, in Latin America commitment to a group is highly valued and in China the focus is on the long term, whereas in the UK and US individualism and short-term results are more important. He also suggested that cultural values influence the way that management is perceived in different countries. In the US managers sell their skills where they can and are cultural heroes – compared to Germany where managers work their way up the ranks and engineers are the cultural heroes.

A managerialist ideology addresses what managers do and how employees and customers should be treated. This includes the following beliefs:

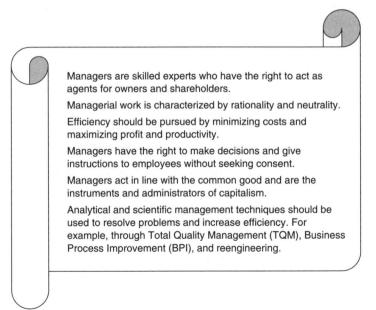

Managers are skilled experts who have the right to act as agents for owners and shareholders.

Managerial work is characterized by rationality and neutrality.

Efficiency should be pursued by minimizing costs and maximizing profit and productivity.

Managers have the right to make decisions and give instructions to employees without seeking consent.

Managers act in line with the common good and are the instruments and administrators of capitalism.

Analytical and scientific management techniques should be used to resolve problems and increase efficiency. For example, through Total Quality Management (TQM), Business Process Improvement (BPI), and reengineering.

Figure 2   Managerialism

These beliefs and practices are regarded as *old managerialism*, in contrast to new forms of managerialism which seem to have taken on a life of their own in government services, education, health care, and other public sector organizations throughout Europe, Australasia and North America. *New managerialism*, or new public management as it is often called, is associated with importing a market orientation and business practices into the public sector as a means of maximizing organizational performance, service and profit through cost-cutting, increased regulation, privatization of services, reengineering and evidence-based management. Jeffrey Pfeffer and Robert Sutton (2006), for example, argue that evidence-based management means making decisions and acting on 'hard facts', which involves: demanding evidence, examining the logic underlying the evidence and any faulty cause-and-effect reasoning, encouraging experimentation to test viability, and reinforcing continuous learning.

Both old and new managerialism are ideological, authoritative, and viewed by some as being oppressive – an issue we will take up in the section on 'destabilization', where we will find managerialism under attack.

professionalization

The Scientific Management, Classical and Human Relations Schools formed the groundwork for legitimizing management as a field of study and as a profession by developing a body of knowledge and expertise around the management of organizations. This body of knowledge provided a basis for establishing formal management qualifications, a system of practice, and professional bodies to regulate and oversee entry, evaluation and promotion to the profession. The first Business School still in existence today, the *École Supérieure de Commerce de Paris* was founded in France 1819,[5] and the first MBA was offered by Harvard Business School in 1910. In 1923 the American Management Association was established, followed by the British Institute of Management in 1947. However, it was the 1960s and 1970s that saw a growth of Management and Organization Studies and the more widespread emergence of Business Schools. Business degrees continued to gain popularity in the 1980s and 1990s[6] across Europe, Asia, Australasia and North America.

From the 1960s onwards, management training also took a hold with the growth of in-company training and development courses and external training and consulting organizations. In the 1990s, corporate universities became popular in US companies such as Motorola, McDonalds and Disney, providing management, leadership, quality and operations training. These developments not only professionalized management, but also established it as a social form and a sought-after career. I began my career in the 1970s working in management training in the gas industry and the National Health Service. We ran numerous courses on the principles of supervision, foundations of management, advanced courses on management and various management topics such as hiring, firing, communicating, motivating and planning. We hired academics to contribute to these courses because they brought a sense of legitimacy to the material. I moved into education, and taught courses leading to certificates, diplomas, masters and Ph.D.s in management, where we drew on a number of empirical studies of management (carried out during the 1960s, 1970s and 1980s) defining the characteristics of managerial work, managerial functions, roles and/or competencies.[7]

There have been many journal articles and a plethora of books, both academic and practitioner-oriented, on the nature of managerial work. But five authors have been particularly influential in contributing to the professionalization of management: Sune Carlson's (1951) study of Swedish executives, Rosemary Stewart's (1967, 1976, 1982) work on UK managers, Henry Mintzberg's (1973) study of CEOs in the US, John Kotter's (1982) and Richard Boyatzis' (1982) studies of US managers. These authors studied what it is that managers do by using a variety of methods including work diaries, interviews, observation, an analysis of contacts and communications, job performance analysis and testing. Their main findings are summarized in Table 1.

Table 1 A comparison of five studies of management

Sune Carlson (1951)	Rosemary Stewart (1967)	Henry Mintzberg (1973)	John Kotter (1982)	Richard Boyatzis (1982)
Executive work	**Managerial work**	**Managerial roles**	**Context, responsibilities and emergent demands**	**Management competencies**
Studied commonalities in executive behaviour. In the work of the CEO: • Geography and location are important. • CEOs operate in a social system and need to consider various perceptions.	Studied how managers spend their time. Activities: • liaising and establishing contacts • maintaining work • innovating and risk taking • setting job boundaries	Studied what managers do. Interpersonal roles: • Figurehead • Leader • Liaison Informational roles: • Monitor • Disseminator • Spokesperson	Studied the behaviour of general managers. Emergent demands: • setting goals, policies, etc. • achieving a delicate balance in allocating resources • keeping on top of complex activities	Characteristics leading to managerial effectiveness. • efficiency orientation: goal and achievement oriented • concern with impact: power and influence • proactive: self-driven • self-confidence: decisive • oral presentation skills

(Cont'd)

Table I

Sune Carlson (1951)	Rosemary Stewart (1967)	Henry Mintzberg (1973)	John Kotter (1982)	Richard Boyatzis (1982)
Pathologies: • wishful thinking • the diary complex • lack of time for undisturbed work • too heavy a workload • inefficient committee organization • unwillingness to establish policies	Context: • demands: what managers must do • constraints: factors limiting activities • choices: opportunities for individual managers to perform differently	Decisional roles: • Entrepreneur • Disturbance handler • Resource allocator • Negotiator	• making decisions in uncertainty • getting information, cooperation and support from bosses, etc. • motivating and controlling a diverse group • implementation of work	• conceptualization: inductive reasoning deductive reasoning • uses socialized power: networks, mobilizes people • manages group processes: encourages teamwork
Key Issue: Identifies administrative pathologies – differences between executive views and actions.	*Key Issue: Identifies the demands, constraints and choices managers face.*	*Key Issue: Focuses on roles as sets of behaviours.*	*Key Issue: Setting agendas*	*Key Issue: Identifies competencies as a basis for training.*

What they found contradicted the classical view of management advocated by Fayol and Taylor, suggesting instead that managerial work is ill-defined and subject to uncertainty, and that management activities are fragmented, involve making choices within constraints, communicating and building networks, and require specific competencies. Underlying much of this work are assumptions that there's an external reality; that organizations exist as structures and systems; that norms and principles govern human behaviour; and that we can identify a set of universal managerial characteristics, roles and competencies that can be generalized across organizations and managers: *realist* assumptions that we'll address in Chapter 2. Within this framework, a manager's reality and identity are created within a social structure, some*thing* s/he has to act within. These assumptions resulted in prescriptive models of managerial work and activities, which formed the basis for establishing a distinct body of management knowledge and expertise.

It's interesting to note that the managerialization and professionalization of Management Studies continued to gain currency – and indeed increase in value – in the US during the 1990s and first decade of the new millennium. Most US Business School curricula continued to centre on the techniques, processes and systems required to increase productivity and efficiency. They were – and are – based on training managers and aspiring managers to become professional master managers. This situation is interesting because during this period of certainty and confidence in capitalism and managerialism in the US, an element of doubt began to creep into European-based Management Studies as we began to recognize that management as both a practice and a body of knowledge is performative: constructed in interaction and through discursive norms and practices, and is therefore contestable. What this means is a recognition that education is not only about preparing us to be good citizens and managers (as managerialism would have us believe), but is also about questioning what seems 'normal', what it means to be a good citizen/manager, and from whose point of view. It also means debating and critiquing different interpretations, and imagining new possibilities. And we didn't really think about critique until we started to draw on ideas from outside Management Studies from the late 1980s onwards. We realized there were some interesting conversations occurring in sociology, cultural anthropology, linguistics and philosophy that raised key questions about what we were doing in our research and teaching as management academics. The issues these questions raised also had implications for management practice. And so the late 1980s and 1990s saw the birth of Critical Management Studies in Europe, and the destabilization of Management Studies.

⬛ ... and so to destabilization

Critical Management Studies (CMS) scholars draw from critical theory, postmodern and poststructuralist theory, critical sociology and linguistics, to unpack and offer alternative understandings of management. Indeed, the very first *Very Short...* book is part of this destabilization process because its purpose was to communicate a critical perspective on organization theory in a more reader-friendly way.[8] While there is a common misconception that CMS means criticizing everything, I suggest this is not the case. CMS is about making the familiar strange and thinking about management differently as a means of opening up possibilities for developing more responsive, creative and ethical ways of managing organizations. While CMS covers a range of issues, concerns and approaches, I suggest there are three main underlying themes of particular relevance to managers and students of management:

- Reality is not what you think it is: the crisis of representation and the constructed nature of managing and organizing.
- Everything is political: ideology critique and the political nature of management.
- Suspicion is on the rise: reflexive approaches to managing.

reality is not what you think it is

In our brief history of management we've seen that over the last century management theory was (and often still is) about making management more scientific and systematic by providing a set of management theories, models, principles and techniques – usually underpinned by a realist ontology. Yet, as we will see, this notion of an objective reality is up for grabs. Cultural anthropologists and sociologists such as James Clifford (1983), George Marcus (with Fischer, 1986), Harold Garfinkel (1967) and Clifford Geertz (1983) questioned our relationship with our social world and the ways in which we account for our experience. They were particularly concerned with asking whether there are 'real' social realities and identities that exist separately from our experience of those realities; whether we experience realities in the same way; and whether we are able to explain – *represent* – social realities accurately and with neutrality. They argued that social realities are constructed as we interact with others and try to make sense of what is going on around us. This brings us to the idea that society and organizations are not pre-existing 'structures', but continually emerge in ongoing interactions and dialogue. Organizational members (including managers) are therefore co-constructors of their organizational realities – whether they realize it or not. This is an idea we will explore further in this and the following chapters.

Knowledge is not immune from this process. Our theories and 'facts' about the world are also socially-constructed, and just as managers have their own situated and contextualized ways of making sense, so do academics. Models of managerial work are created by researchers about what *the researcher* thinks it is that the managers in their study are doing. And there's a performative issue here, because the so-called objective, simplified academic model is often viewed as the reality, and our perceptions of social practices are filtered through, and reinforce, these models as we seek patterns of behaviour that fit the categories identified in the model. CMS scholars are interested in destabilizing and exploring categorizations, and examining the potential consequences of taken-for-granted notions of organization and management. This is often with the aim of examining alternative conceptualizations and practices.

everything is political

One branch of CMS lies within poststructuralism, where scholars use a Foucauldian perspective to argue that realities and subjectivities are constructed both by discursive practices (linguistic systems and ways of talking, texts, ways of thinking, etc.) and non-discursive practices (institutional structures, social practices, techniques, etc.) that regulate what we accept as 'normal' and what we do not. We are often unaware of this normalizing process because we are products of it – it's only when we move into a different context, for example another organization, or if a new colleague starts to question us, that we realize what it is that we take for granted. Knowledge plays a disciplining role in this process because it consists of unconscious rules and practices that determine what is 'good' knowledge; what are 'good' standards for judgement; who are experts; and therefore who can control meaning and speak for others. So a Foucauldian branch of CMS examines the power relationships and disciplinary forms of surveillance existing within organizational settings.

These normalizing and disciplinary practices are riddled with power because they privilege particular ideologies, social structures, institutional practices and groups over others (Foucault, 1970, 1972). Capitalism and managerialism are examples of ideologies that are subject to critique: a critique reflected in a second branch of CMS based on Marxist and neo-Marxist analyses of the politics of capitalism, organization and work. Within this branch of work, critical theorists and labour process theorists examine the various forms of control that privilege elite groups of owners, shareholders and managers, and lead to the domination of other groups. One of the issues studied by critical theorists is why workers willingly consent to their own exploitation and accept this exploitation as 'normal', and how, on the other hand, they might resist this exploitation. Labour process theorists argue that managers control workers by systematically de-skilling work so that workers can be easily replaced. We'll explore these aspects of power further in Chapter 3.

CMS also destabilizes the ideologies of managerialism and new managerialism by asking us to think about them in different ways. Mark Learmonth and Nancy Harding (2006) for example, argue that evidence-based management constructs what are seen as facts and data in a particular way, thus privileging specific forms of evidence over others. This in turn perpetuates the domination of some groups by others. They are not suggesting we throw evidence out, but that we broaden what we consider to be evidence. A number of CMS scholars focus on the role that Business Schools play in perpetuating a managerialist ideology. Some have suggested that MBA programmes are market-driven commodities in which faculty are producers and students are consumers needing to be satisfied, and that we need a critical pedagogy of practice in which students question taken-for-granted practices, reconstruct themselves as managers, and 'rethink the purpose of' their organizations (Welsh and Dehler, 2007).

A third branch of CMS that draws from cultural studies is that of postcolonialism. It is of particular interest because of the globalization of business and the increasing influence of multinational corporations. I mentioned earlier the notion that Management Studies is westernized and ethnocentric, something we often take for granted. For example, we often teach westernized management techniques and practices to multicultural classes with international students. Such techniques can be tools of colonialism, an imposition of culture and an exploitation of the people, material and economic resources of the colonized country. Postcolonialist scholars, particularly Edward Said (1993) and Homi Bhabha (1994), argued that this privileges the colonizer's (assumed to be more civilized) culture as the right worldview, the right rationality, set of values, way of behaving, etc., to the detriment of other experiences, other forms of knowledge and other voices. This has obvious implications for managing global organizations because, postcolonialists argue, powerful multinational corporations have spearheaded the homogenization of different cultures into one westernized global culture that has disenfranchised and impoverished many people. This assimilation of different cultures has become known as the McDonaldization or Disneyfication of culture.[9] Rupa Thadhani (2005) suggests that postcolonialism recognizes and builds on the plurality of different values, perspectives, narratives and identities.

suspicion is on the rise

A third CMS critique argues that much of management studies to date is not only managerialistic, therefore privileging the few, but is also reductionist in the sense of trying to simplify a complex, ideological, political and social process to a set of principles, roles and techniques justified by a supposed rationality. This knowledge is packaged for consumers to take away and use: transferred from the computer of a faculty member to that of a student, along with a certificate of completion. This might sound cynical, but the advent of on-line degrees and courses facilitates this process.

However, if you believe that management and managers have an impact on not just how people are treated in their immediate organization, but on the community and society at large, then critical thinking, moral debate, alternative and imaginative ways of thinking are key to managing organizations in responsible and responsive ways. Managers need to consider their role and responsibility in society; to consider not just the means of managing (the techniques), but the ends and the outcomes. I am suggesting that managing is subject to political enactments, and is both a relational and a moral practice.

But CMS is not just suspicious about conventional management knowledge and practice – it should also be suspicious about itself. In other words, as CMS scholars we should walk the talk and question our own assumptions and practices if we believe knowledge is constructed, contested and speculative – because *all* forms of knowledge, whether conventional or critical, are constructed.

In *Against Management* (2002), Martin Parker argues that CMS is basically a debate that takes place within the cloistered halls of academia and has had little impact on practice. But I suggest that it really depends upon how you teach CMS and whether you can engage management students in thinking differently about their experience. As managers and aspiring managers, students are often deeply enmeshed in prevailing managerial ideologies, structures of control and systems of power. And their career depends upon maintaining this system. CMS offers managers a basis for thinking differently about themselves and their organizational experience. It's this different way of thinking – about social and organizational life as emergent, socially constructed, and inherently ideological and political – that encourages managers to challenge taken-for-granted organizational realities, places upon them a responsibility for relationships with others, and forms the genesis for alternative realities. As one of my Exec MBA students commented after completing a leadership course taught from a critical and a phenomenological perspective:

Regarding your class...

I was a bit surprised that I actually enjoyed it. When I saw the syllabus, I was fairly certain I wouldn't get much out of it. Don't get me wrong, I still dislike writing long academic essays and cramming a ton of difficult reading into a few short weeks. But I probably never would have read [the course readings] on my own – I really enjoyed it and it helped me through some rough times these past few months ... I think you were the only professor in the program who actually encouraged open dissent ... It was very refreshing.[10]

CMS does have something practical to offer managers – but it's a different practicality to the norm of technical rationality so prevalent in many Business Schools. It's a practicality based on the critical questioning of taken-for-granted practices and their impact, and it involves questioning not just the means of management, but also its ends.

what or who are managers?

A review of the literature on the nature of managerial work and managerial identities reveals a range of approaches, underpinned by assumptions from realism to social constructionism, determinism to free will, and coherence to fragmented and free-floating realities and identities. At the risk of oversimplifying, these approaches relate to whether the authors believe:

- That we can discover a universal and unified definition of managerial identity (realism) or that managerial identities are socially and/or linguistically constructed and therefore relative to time, place and personal experience.
- That the manager is a passive instrument on which identity or cultural meanings are inscribed, or she/he exercises free will and interpretive choice in deciding what to do and who to be.
- Managerial identity is a social, an individual, or a relational attribute.
- Managerial identities are coherent, contested, or somewhere in-between.

Where you fall on these issues will influence not just your conceptualization of management, but also how you manage. Table 1 highlights some of the earlier studies, which tend to view identity from a realist, mainly passive, coherent and socially attributed or determined perspective. A number of the more contemporary studies have taken a constructed and contested view, discovering that even managers themselves find it difficult to define their identity and articulate what it is that they do (e.g., Thomas and Linstead, 2002; Watson and Harris, 1999). Tony Watson and Pauline Harris suggest this social opaqueness means managerial identities are always emerging, and management is a social process in which managers make 'their worlds at the same time as their worlds are making them' (1999: 238). Thus manager's identities are precarious and managers often feel insecure and vulnerable.

Let's have a look at some of the different ways of talking about and constructing managers.

managers as rational agents

Ra·tion·al (adj): Able to think clearly and sensibly, because the mind is not impaired by physical or mental condition, violent emotion, or prejudice.[11]

As we have seen, the twentieth century was dominated by rational models, which were situated within a realist perspective and attempted to define the characteristics of managerial work, managerial functions, activities, roles and competencies. These models began with the work of early organizational and administrative theorists, both academics and practitioners, who were concerned about bringing the logic of technical rationality, systematization and objectivity to management. And students on management courses often want to know what is the right answer, the right way of doing something, and how to get to the 'truth' ... because to be rational is to be right and to be credible. Rationality is the basis for managerial power and legitimacy, and includes calculative techniques of measurement and control. In 1924, Max Weber talked about rational-legal authority as essential to the ideal form of organization – bureaucracy. Early approaches to motivation were based on the notion of 'rational economic man', a perfectly informed individual who makes choices based on weighing the costs and benefits of each course of action, and is motivated by money (recall Frederick Taylor's work). This notion was later challenged by Herbert Simon (1955), who said that in reality, we rationally adjust because we work within constraints that mean that perfect rationality is impossible. The best we can hope for is a rationality bounded by constraints such as imperfect information: nevertheless, still a form of rationality.

Within this frame, managers are rational agents acting in the best interest of owners and shareholders. Indeed, behavioural economists and accountants developed agency theory to explain how to ensure management acts in the best interest of owners and shareholders. A theory that originated and initially developed in America (see Kathleen Eisenhardt's 1989 review), agency theory is about the rights of managers to control. It is based on the idea that the relationship between a principal (an owner, stockholders, etc.) and an agent (someone hired to perform the work, for example a manager) is potentially problematic because both will have different goals. So the principal must minimize the risk in the relationship and be certain that the agent will achieve organizational goals in the most efficient way and carry out the work to the best of his or her ability. How? Mainly by the application of rational management techniques such as information systems, budgetary controls and performance management systems. You might note that these all relate to monitoring and controlling performance.

Much of management practice, research and management education is based on the principle of rationality. Charles Kepner and Benjamin Tregoe (1965) published *The Rational Manager*, an influential text that identified a rational process of decision-making. There's now a Kepner–Tregoe worldwide consulting organization offering solutions to human and organizational problems. This is achieved through the KT Way®, which focuses on reaching the right decision through rational thinking (with emotion and subjectivity removed), and a rational process of situational appraisal, problem analysis, decision analysis, and potential problem (opportunity) analysis. As is typical of rational management, they state that these processes are 'universally applicable, regardless of cultural setting or content'.[12]

Yet rationality is contested both conceptually and practically. If there *is* one rationality, then we wouldn't have disagreement and conflict. We'd all come to the same conclusion and organizations would run perfectly – unless of course you have to deal with 'irrational' people who are not objective and make decisions based on value judgements! And yes, this statement is made tongue-in-cheek, because it raises the question 'Whose rationality is the right one?' The contested nature of rationality can be seen in a 2008 article on 'How Apple got everything right by doing everything wrong', in which Leander Kahney talks about CEO Steve Jobs' counter-rationality and includes the following quote: '"Steve proves that it's OK to be an asshole," says Guy Kawasaki, Apple's former chief evangelist. "I can't relate to the way he does things, but it's not his problem. It's mine. He just has a different OS."' I'm not advocating that managers be assholes – I'm merely pointing out that there's more than one 'operating system' or rationality. That what might seem perfectly rational to the manager making a decision, may seem irrational to the person implementing the decision. In addition, rationality, as Gareth Morgan (2006) says is political, because managers use rationality to justify and achieve their own personal, work and career interests. Having worked in a number of organizations, both business and academic, I find from experience that what is rational to one person is often not rational to others. On a day-to-day basis, organizations encompass many different rationalities. And maybe it's just me, but I have never been able to successfully apply the seven principles of a more organized life, the ten steps to fitness, or the five stages to financial and/or career success because life is not that simple (or perhaps I'm just trying to rationalize my non-rationality?!).

Another major critique is that rationality carries a subtext of binary oppositions:

Rational / Non-rational
Control / Chaos
Intellectual / Emotional
Neutral / Subjective
Mind / Body
Male / Female

French philosopher Derrida (1978) argues that words derive their meaning from their opposite, for example, good/bad, male/female, organization/disorganization. So when you use one term (e.g., true), you are implicitly drawing on its opposite (false), and in doing so you are privileging one term over the other, making one better than the other. The privileged term becomes an unquestioned norm, which then favours one group over others. What this means is that managers can use the term 'rational', intentionally or otherwise, to justify their interests and legitimate their authority, because being rational is good and right whereas being 'irrational' (or not subscribing to one particular version of rationality) is wrong. *Rationality is thus based on who has the power to decide what is rational* – an issue we'll explore further in Chapter 3.

managers as actors

A contrasting notion to that of managers as rational agents, is that of managers as actors. This draws on Erving Goffman's (1959, 1961, 1967) work on dramaturgy, the idea that we are all actors engaged in ongoing performances of the real and of our identity. We draw on a range of cues, pre-existing scripted behaviours and roles, within a particular physical setting. From a dramaturgical perspective, organizations are social dramas or 'theatres' consisting of many different performances coordinated to achieve organizational goals. Managers are actors managing these performances and defining the roles and scripts of others. Individuals and teams cooperate in performances and follow routines: pre-established patterns of action. Front stage is a regular 'official' performance with often very routinized and symbolic actions, where we manage the impressions of others through our appearance, actions, language and so on, and where both actors and audience collaborate to maintain the situation. Backstage performances are behind-the-scenes preparations and conversations. Goffman suggests while performing we act into prior realities but also influence and manage those realities. So, for example, a front stage performance might involve managers planning and presenting a united stance regarding the necessary implementation of a new performance management programme, while backstage expressing their doubts about its efficacy. Front stage performances should be coherent, any dissent being relegated to backstage. Any deviants from the front stage norm are often marginalized.

For Goffman, identity is a *dramatic realization* of a social role, consistent with social norms and expectations. So from a dramaturgical perspective, managers as actors see front stage performances as strategic interactions in which they deliberately act their identity to maintain a common managerial role, define the situation for the audience, present a *face* or *mask* (an image of oneself in this context), and avoid losing face. Ian Greener (2007) found within the UK National Health Service that while clinician power had been eroded over the previous 20 years, senior managers collaborated in a performance to conceal this shift of power to allow clinicians to believe they were still in charge – to save face. The senior managers achieved their agendas by paying deference to clinicians and getting their agreement on issues front stage – this meant that clinicians thought they were still in charge and yet would lose face if they didn't comply with decisions. NHS managers were therefore acting out their identity within pre-scribed scripts, yet also improvising to achieve their agendas.

Managing in a dramaturgical context means creating a play (or a series of plays) with plots, various scenes and characters or roles for organizational members. Isn't this idea rather far-fetched? Maybe not – I put on my suit (costume) to come to work, I interact with people at work differently from the way I interact with friends and family (front stage compared to backstage), I set goals and plans to achieve those goals (plots), talk to peers about how to present an idea or a change in work systems to members of staff (a scene), create job descriptions and person specifications (character), etc. This also involves *impression management*, presenting a positive social identity to others. In Goffman's sense, managers are actors involved in impression management: presenting themselves as credible managers and successfully staging managerial performances. The relationship between impression management, language and identity was noted by one of my students:

> During my early days as a manager the one item I found most difficult was that of language. I pride myself on being an extremely honest person and truly believe in what DS [a guest speaker] told us, 'Without trust societies and economies fall apart.' My early observations of other leaders, was their tendency to use words that often seemed misleading. Instead of admitting to the mistake of over-hiring staff they would emphasize their frugalness in performing layoffs. Instead of confessing that they made a bad hire they would characterize the terminated manager as a disappointment to all

senior management. In hindsight, these managers were choosing their words carefully, or framing, in an attempt to define a reality different to that I saw. I found it difficult to participate in what I considered dishonest games...

As well as performing a coherent front stage performance, these managers were also engaged in face-saving, which caused a personal dilemma regarding conformity for my student who later found himself overlooked in a management reorganization.

Of course this raises the question as to whether managers are being disingenuous in their relationships with others, or whether they are savvy manipulators? From a managerialist perspective, impression management is just part of the repertoire of tools available to ensure the achievement of organizational goals. On the other hand, Heather Höpfl (2002) argues that acting a part in an organizational performance, whether as a manager or employee, requires the 'good' actor to submit herself to, while detaching herself from, the performance. She says that this results in a performed hypocrisy, especially in service jobs where one has to act a particular way for customers. For example, for a short time my daughter had a job as a teller in a US Bank. Her manager told her that she had to learn to smile more 'authentically' and to better project the 'WOW! factor' to customers, which Lauren felt meant being overly perky and inauthentic – something she just couldn't do! Höpfl says such performed hypocrisy can lead to emotional stress for actors forced to play a role, and to estrangement, degradation and contempt.

managers of meaning: storytellers

The idea that managers are managers of meaning comes from a different tradition to that of Goffman's performance. Both relate to the notion that we construct our social realities in our interaction, but whereas Goffman sees performance as a collaborative, ritualistic, more-or-less prescribed and deliberate performance, managing meaning involves a greater degree of spontaneity, responsiveness to our surroundings and individuality, in the sense that our personal life history also influences our identity. The management of meaning tends to draw from Karl Weick's (1995) work on sensemaking and from a narrative tradition. It also emphasizes the importance of language in shaping meaning and organizing action.

Let's begin with Weick, who over the last 30 years has done much to develop the notion of sensemaking in organizational life. Weick sees sensemaking as *committed interpretation*. He says our actions and interactions are usually in situations where there are social commitments to act, and where our actions also create social commitments. For example, managers behave in particular ways towards employees because ... it's their role, their boss/subordinate expects them to, the organization requires it, because they've been trained to do so ... and so on. Sensemaking is about picking up cues and clues in situations, of being able to see and create (talk into being) a coherent story of events. For Weick, this is how organizations and identities are enacted. For example, when a manager is asked in a meeting how quality improvements can be made to a product, she may call on knowledge, intuition, experience, beliefs and new ideas to respond. This is not performing a script, but involves a 'willingness to forgo planning and rehearsing in favor of acting in real time' (2001: 299). He says that if we are overly concerned with technique, then we are often poor improvisers, and because managers have to deal with ambiguities, uncertainties, contradictions and discontinuities, they need to improvise.

Gowler and Legge (1996) expand on what they call the anthropological aspect of the management of meaning, the idea that as managers talk, they are not only communicating meaning, but also creating and maintaining culture. They do so by shifting between plain talk and rhetoric – symbolic, poetic and emotional forms of speaking. Let me illustrate this with a brief excerpt from a conversation I had with the Vice President of a US Public Utility:

> My job has turned to high risk since deregulation – even though it is still highly regulated. Before it was real easy. Now I feel like Paul Revere's horse – it was the horse that ran from Charlestown to Lexington – Paul yelled – nobody remembers the horse! That's the way I feel! [laughter]

Notice the shift from plain talk about 'deregulation' to rhetoric: it was the rhetoric that connected and gave me a sense of how he felt. His words also generated a much more powerful and lasting response from me than if he had said, 'I get little recognition' – I sympathized with his feeling of being unrecognized. Rhetoric can be powerful in shaping meaning.

A number of authors have extended the notion of sensemaking to storytelling in management. Creating a story is seen as a way of creating meaning about our experience and our lives, and also a way of shaping action. David Boje (1991, 1995) has studied storytelling in organizations over a number of years. He argues that storytelling is a way for organizational members to make sense of the past, present and future and to cope with change, because stories provide some continuity with the past, and also help fashion the future. Managers create and tell stories about organizational events, people or heroes to connect employees with organizational culture and ways of doing things. Stories are also ways of making sense, of handling the hurt of organizational experience (Watson, 2001). So good managers are good storytellers. There's a great example of this on YouTube, where a 28-year-old Steve Jobs 'performs' his 1983 Apple keynote speech, introduces the by now classic 1984 Macintosh advert, and re-energizes a demotivated sales force.[13] It's well worth watching. Notice the music, the build-up of the story of a heroic Apple versus the monolithic IBM, the symbolism and rhetoric of the Mac TV advert, and the response of the audience. A masterful manager of meaning!

Managers often tell stories in their everyday conversations. I noticed in one of my conversations with a Vice President of a Health Care organization that he told a lot of stories. I'd ask him to explain something, and he'd tell a story. When I commented on this, he responded:

MIKE: and I do a lot of that. For me probably the most effective way in dialogue is to tell stories and use analogies and to make pictures ...

ANN: ... it can be very persuasive ...

MIKE: Yes, I think comments about it being the weakest form of argument is probably a very modernist view you know. Clearly, when one is trained and educated in the sixties/seventies, you know, right in the teeth of rationalism, it sticks [*laughter*]. But by native style I'm much more a storyteller. Matter of fact sometimes for presentations I've written fables and presented ... a particular Board of Directors – I remember we were struggling with an issue about strategy and where do we go, and they had a very difficult time seeing themselves in the picture – right? – and what they were causing to happen in the organization. And so I wrote this about 6–8 page fable and read it at the board meeting, about the Middle Ages, and likened our organization to a marauding band that had to support itself off the land at the same time it was trying to ... and they got it! They could find themselves! And it was very helpful.

ANN: Did they make those connections with themselves?

MIKE: Oh yes, it wasn't subtle [*laughter*]. It just moved it out into a safer context in which for them to see themselves, for them to say this is what we're doing. Is this a problem we're causing...?[14]

So in this example, the Vice President was not only a natural story-teller, in that it was part of his way of communicating meaning, but he used stories deliberately as a trigger to try to get his Board of Directors to see the implications and potential consequences of their decisions in a very different way.

David Sims (2003) suggests that stories are sense-making devices, making sense of our surroundings for others, but also storying our own lives: narrating our identity to ourselves and to others. What this means is that we try to make sense of our lives – to ourselves and to others – by creating some sort of coherent narrative or story in which we are the main character, someone who has particular qualities. A colleague might ask us why we made a decision or acted in a particular way, so we explain by pulling together and connecting what we see as all the events, reasons, feelings, who said what to whom etc., to *narrate* or give an account of our action. This is one small part of narrating our life into some sort of sense, and from a manager's perspective the narration might involve creating our character and establishing our credibility as a manager. But Sims says this always involves a degree of uncertainty because our stories can be contested or ignored by others. He argues that middle managers are particularly vulnerable because they are in career transition and have to deal with the differing expectations of senior management and subordinates – and both expect 'good' stories that are meaningful and hold their attention. However, middle managers often find themselves telling stories to subordinates that they themselves do not believe, or stories that later may be publicly discredited by senior management. So they are constantly trying to save face and maintain a sense of identity.

David Boje develops this notion of contested stories at an organizational level. His postmodern analysis focuses on the oppressive and disciplinary aspects of storytelling, arguing that organizations can be turned into warring factions or collectives as different groups create their own stories and attempt to recruit supporters (Boje, 1994; Boje and Rosile, 1997). Consider the situation where there is no coherent organizational story, and the conflict that can occur between departments who have their own agendas or storylines and see each other as rivals to be discredited.

Finally, it's interesting to note that storytelling has become commodified – a Marxist idea in which something is given economic value in the market. In this case, whereas storytelling is a natural part of everyday interaction, it has now become a product to be sold and to be consumed by others. I came across a 2005 web article describing how US company EDS brought in a UK consulting company, The Storytellers, to help the company bring back a tradition of storytelling started by its founder, Ross Perot.[15] The company felt that storytelling would plot the company's strategy journey, reconnect employees to the senior management and engage them with the organization's vision. Managers were trained in the company story, but given some leeway to create their own stories around the company's story maps. A similar storytelling strategy has also been used by the UK company Parcelforce. While stories, symbols and rhetoric can be powerful in helping create meaning and connection with an organization's culture and history, employees do recognize when stories are authentic. Managing meaning means not only understanding the importance of language, symbols and spontaneity (or improvisation), but also the importance of integrity and sincerity.

managers as discursive subjectivities

Let's begin with what is meant by 'discursive subjectivities'. This perspective draws on poststructuralist thought which, as we will see in the next chapter, addresses how language (discourse with a small 'd') and language systems (Discourse with a capital 'D') shape realities that are image-driven, contradictory, fragmented, elusive and power-ridden. So scholars taking a D/discursive approach, study the relationship between language use, social action and social theory. In terms of management, this means examining how talk, written text, physical and symbolic artifacts, and broader social, historical, economic and ideological forces shape management theory, practice and identity. Many poststructural studies draw on the work of Michel Foucault (1980, 1988), who argued that the subject (identity) is the product of various discourses and forms of knowledge. In Foucauldian terms, D/discourse categorizes the individual and is inscribed on our bodies – structuring our behaviour, desires and ways of talking. This turns us into a *subjectivity*, a site where D/discourses of power and control meet and organize identity, and in the process create conflict by subjecting us to forces and practices with which we may disagree and may either conform or try to resist.

So from a poststructural perspective managerial subjectivity is performative, but in a different sense from Goffman's performance. In *Bodies That Matter* (1993), Judith Butler differentiates the two: performing is a conscious performance of a ritual, while performativity is concealed in performance and is discursive – a powerful form of speech that produces actions and an *unconscious* reiteration of a norm or social category.

Subjectivities are also multiple and fragmented as different D/discourses create competing pressures. Alison Pullen (2006) examines the subjective identities of middle managers within broader social discourses and gendered organizational discourses, arguing that managers' identities are sites of negotiation and contestation. Let's take a hypothetical example to see how managers can be viewed as discursive subjectivities:

> You work in XL as a middle manager. The company currently stresses transformational leadership, performance metrics, organizational agility, and creative partnering, as expressed in the company value statement. These are four significant organizational discourses reinforced by the CEO's speeches to the media, and in meetings with senior managers and middle managers (discourse). You have been through programmes training you to be visionary, charismatic and proactive; how to control department costs and performance through measurement; how to monitor and adapt quickly to technological advancements and market changes; and how to be more

flexible in working across department boundaries to improve productivity and quality. Yet managers are evaluated and rewarded individually on whether his or her department is under budget, and whether they have met production targets on time. Five years ago you had the authority to do what it took to make something happen, but now you have to get pre-approval for anything that involves expenditure over £500, and the process can take anything from six months to a year depending on the amount of justification required by senior management...

The four organizational discourses, along with discursive practices such as training, appraisal and information systems, shape the identities of managers by requiring specific actions and behaviours. You have to make choices about what to do and which identity to take at any particular moment in time: an inspirer of others, an enforcer of performance standards for individual employees, an innovator who is subject to close controls, and a collaborator with others as and when needed. You are frustrated trying to balance the demands of each, by trying to be proactive while feeling like a puppet because you have no authority and spend your time producing statistics. You try to remain positive with your staff, while remaining distant from your boss who trots out the company line. Most middle managers just keep their heads down and focus on meeting short-term goals, while complaining to each other about conflicting demands. Some are deliberately uncooperative, and refuse to attend any more training sessions. You feel torn in different directions and struggle to find a sense of coherence, and find yourself becoming less and less committed to the organization ...

This example is an attempt to show how managers can be constructed as multiple and fragmented subjectivities – as effects of D/discursive processes, tossed between contested meanings and shifting fields of power which they accept but also passively resist. I've taken some liberties in this example, because I've given my manager (the 'you' of the story) a self-consciousness that many poststructuralists would deny in favour of a subject who is an 'it', or an effect of discourse. In addition, one of the major debates in what is known as the discursive turn in organization studies, is the degree to which we are just dupes of D/discursive practices, whether we can be creative in resisting imposed identities, or if we are somewhere in-between as simultaneously consentors and resisters. In my scenario, some managers are the latter, trying to negotiate the demands of competing discourses.

There have been a number of studies of managers as discursive subjectivities, but a couple you may find particularly interesting are Sveningsson and Alvesson's (2003) study of managerial identity, and Gail Fairhurst's (2007) study of how leadership is D/discursively constructed. Viewing managers as discursive subjectivities can offer a different way of thinking about what, or who, managers are and how managers relate to their surroundings.

managers as practical authors

The notion of managers as practical authors was first outlined in 1993 by John Shotter in his book *Conversational Realities*, and later developed by myself (2001) along with John (2002). Drawing on social constructionist assumptions, we see managers not as rational problem solvers, but as authors – with other organizational participants – of their organization's social realities. Why authors? Well, this brings us to the idea that we create and maintain our organizational 'realities', policies, procedures and practices in our interaction and our everyday conversations with others. Shotter says that organizations are indeterminate and ill-defined realms of activity – a chaotic welter of impressions. Indeed, when you ask managers about their organizational lives, they rarely talk about structures, roles, scripts or performances, but about those ill-defined aspects: about feeling pushed or pulled in different directions, the dilemmas they face in terms of who they are and what to say or do. Managers are continually trying to make sense of this chaotic welter of impressions and the many voices (Bakhtin's heteroglossia, pp. 73–5 below) in the organizational landscape, and in doing so they are shaping the organization's social landscape by negotiating some kind of shared meaning, and by creating new possibilities for moving forward and for coordinating actions. They turn, as Shotter says, the imaginary into the imagined. Think of the imaginary as something tacit, not articulated or well understood yet influencing our actions and talk in implicit ways – while the imagined is articulated as a shared, ongoing languaged activity that orders our actions and talk.

But how does this occur? It occurs through the language we use, what we say, and *how* we say it. But practical authorship goes beyond the words used to a different way of thinking about managing as a relational process. If we accept that we shape realities and identities *between* us, that we do not live, act and talk in isolation but always in relation to others whether they are present or not, then managing is a dialogic (multi-voiced) relationship of creating meaning and action *with others in relationally responsive interaction*. But because managers have influence, they play a crucial role in authoring organizational realities and identities. This re-visions mana*ging* as a continually emerging, embodied practice, *a way of being and relating*, rather than the conventional view of management as a series of disembodied activities or roles within an already existing reality. Thus, managing is about who we are, because our actions, our ways of making sense and constructing our world are not separate from us, they do not stem from a detached knowledge of the world, but are intimately linked to what we feel, say, and how we engage with our surroundings. As Tony Watson says, managers 'continually "work on" their humanness' (2001: 19), that is, *who they are* as they relate and converse with people. As one manager commented to me:

> Jeff: I tend to be more of a … strategist, not someone who's down mucking around in all the details – although I do that to a certain extent … I've spent some time down on the production floor talking to the line employees – I don't do a lot of that … I don't know … I try and walk through. But basically it's the other seven members of the management team and the first line supervisors, and the physical plant people – maintenance personnel, they're the main people I talk to … it's the only way I know of I can keep my hand on the big picture – and the thought of losing the big picture, to me, is catastrophic!

We can infer from Jeff's comments that he sees himself as always in conversational relationships with others, and that he's acting from, while working on, his own sense of self as he talks with people. Within authorship, talk and action, self and others are interwoven, and therefore it's important for managers to consider *how* they relate with others. This means thinking about the assumptions they hold about people, understanding how others may view the world, and creating opportunities for open dialogue – which brings us to another way of constructing managers.

managers as reflexive practitioners

Over the last ten years or so one of my interests has been in developing the notion of managers as reflexive practitioners. In fact, this is what much of this book is about. While management education emphasizes the need for reflection, few programmes move towards what I believe is fundamental to managing organizations in responsive, responsible and ethical ways – reflexivity. And it's reflexivity that is key to understanding management in terms of *who managers are*. So let me begin by explaining the difference between reflection and reflexivity.

One of the earliest and probably best known authors in the field of reflection, is John Dewey, who in a book originally published in 1910, was concerned with the role of reflection in broadening critical thinking skills. Dewey argued that the aim of education is a logically trained mind, and that central to this is reflection, which involves a balance between analysis and synthesis, concrete and abstract, and between experiential and experimental (empirical and scientific) thinking. A disciplined mind involves an 'ability to "turn things over," to look at matters deliberately, to judge whether the amount and kind of evidence requisite for decision is at hand' (Dewey, 1997 [1910]: 66–7). This was further reinforced by Donald Schön (1983), who argued that competent professionals engage in reflective practice as a means of dealing with complex and uncertain situations. They do so by *reflecting-in-action*, engaging in a reflective conversation and constructing an understanding of the situation using a repertoire of personal experience and situational knowledge. This reflective conversation involves framing and reframing the problem, finding new meanings in the situation, and judging the possible impact of alternative courses of action.

Reflection is based on a realist view of the world, that there is a reality to be discovered and concrete objects we can think about, measure, categorize and develop theory to explain. Reflection is also associated with assumptions of a rational and reasoning being with an inner consciousness, making logical sense and developing a set of accurate statements about an outside world. It's viewed as a cognitive or intellectual activity in which being reflective means thinking about something in an objective, logical and neutral way.

Reflexivity draws on a social constructionist view of the world. As John Shotter says, 'Social constructionists loop the circle of reflexivity around onto themselves. From our point of view, it thus becomes a problem as to why, at this moment in history, we account for our experience of ourselves in the way we do' (1992: 177). In other words, reflexivity goes deeper than reflection, because it means interrogating the taken-for-granted by questioning our relationship with our social world and the ways in which we account for our experience. We've begun the journey in this chapter by looking at the different ways in which management and managers are constructed, and we'll continue it in Chapter 2 by examining conventional ways of thinking about the relationship between the world, language, communication and management. Managers as reflexive practitioners believe that we shape our social and organizational realities between us in our everyday interactions, and routinely engage in questioning this process.

Elsewhere, I've suggested that reflexivity is situated in constructionist and deconstructionist approaches, and that the former can be linked to self reflexivity, the latter to critically reflexive practice. Table 2 summarizes the main assumptions of each approach.

Reflexive practitioners engage in both. But what does this mean? Being *self reflexive* means questioning our own ways of being, relating and acting. It means thinking about how, in our living conversation with others, our assumptions, words and responses influence meaning and help shape 'organizational realities'. In doing so, we question the limitations of our assumptions and our sensemaking; whether we respond defensively or openly to people; and the multiplicity of meanings and voices we may or may not hear in our relationships and interactions with others. Being self reflexive forms a basis for exploring how we may personally act in responsible and ethical ways.

Table 2   Assumptions underlying reflexivity

Constructionist	Deconstructionist
Social and organizational realities: Emerge in everyday conversational and discursive activities. 'Realities' are shaped and maintained in language use. Organizations are language communities and/or communities of social practices.	**Social and organizational realities:** Constructed through discursive and non-discursive practices. 'Realities' are fragmented, fleeting, and contested. Organizations are discursively constructed sites of power, discipline, normalization, marginalization and resistance.
Self: Selves and identities are shaped in everyday interaction.	**Self:** A subject constructed and normalized through discursive practices.
Language: What we say, and how we say it, shapes meaning and creates and reproduces social realities.	**Language:** The separation of words and objects. Meaning is constantly deferred and constructed through binary oppositions.
Knowledge: An implicit and indexical knowing, sense-making within contexts, knowledge as interpretation and insight.	**Knowledge:** A political process of the production of temporary texts, 'facts' and 'truths', and the consumption of such texts.

Constructionist	Deconstructionist
Self-reflexivity:	**Critical-reflexivity:**
Exposing the situated, tentative and provisional nature of our social and organizational realities and knowledge.	Destabilizing and deconstructing Truths, ideologies, language, overarching narratives, single
Exploring how we constitute our social and organizational experience and identities in everyday interaction.	meanings, authority, and disciplinary practices. Revealing and interrogating assumptions
Exploring multiple meanings and interpretations.	that privilege particular groups.

Source: After Cunliffe, 2009.

Critical reflexivity draws from critical theory, poststructural and postmodern commitments to unsettle the assumptions underlying theoretical, ideological and relational (or practical) positions. Thus we begin to think more critically about social and organizational policies and practices. This means complicating rather than simplifying, questioning rather than answering or accepting, looking for paradoxes and contradictions rather than order and patterns, thinking about what lies unsaid as well as what is said, and recognizing multiple perspectives rather than imposing an ideology or worldview. Critically reflexive managers examine the assumption that there's one rational way of managing organizations and that decisions can be justified solely on the basis of efficiency and profit. They question 'normal' taken-for-granted strategies, policies, programmes and organizational practices as a basis for understanding how and why these practices might impact people and exclude them from active participation in organizational life. This is with the aim of creating more critical and open dialogue, and more responsive and ethical organizations. Self and critical reflexivity are crucially tied to ethical management and leadership.

I often find when discussing the relevance of reflexivity with managers, that their initial response is – we can't question everything all of the time or we'd *never* get anything done. I agree. It's about knowing what's important to question, and being aware of how we relate to others. As one manager says:

> ... by caring, by empathizing, by questioning the assumptions behind systems, and by keeping an eye on what is truly important. That's a challenge for me. My experience, in 25 years at — Corporation, is that many of those systems have contributed to the success of one of the most successful companies in US history. But there *are* two ends of the 'manage' spectrum ... (Cunliffe, 2001). Manag*ing* and manag*ement*. Manag*ing* is a way of being and relating – a continually emerging, embodied practice. Manag*ement* is a series of disembodied activities. And balancing the two, I believe, is critical: just as it is in the implementation of any philosophy, system or habit. A leader can spend too much time on facts and details, concrete steps of implementation, HR policies and procedures and the like. A leader can also overly focus on being philosophic – to the neglect of proven leadership tools, principles and techniques as taught by the likes of

Peter Drucker and Henry Mintzberg. So maintaining a balance is important...

Managers as reflexive practitioners think about social and organizational life as emergent, socially constructed and inherently ideological and political. They challenge taken-for-granted organizational realities and, in doing so, emphasize their responsibility for managing in more responsive ways and helping shape new, more collaborative and inclusive forms of reality.[16]

summary

The purpose of this chapter has been to look at some of the different ways that management and managers have been constructed over the years. This history not only helps explain the current focus of management education and practice, but also illustrates its performative nature – that management and managerial identities have come into being through the various management Discourses and through the everyday practices of managers. Why is this important? Because even though our ideas about what management should be are historically, culturally and linguistically influenced, if we believe management is also shaped in interaction, and that one is always *becoming a manager*, then management and managerial identities are open to reinvention. The more contemporary ways of viewing managers, as practical authors, managers of meaning and reflexive practitioners, offer not only a different way of thinking about what managers do and who they are, but also a different way of performing or *doing* management. Foundational ways of framing management as rational, neutral and legitimate constrain both managerial action and identities (think of the impact of traditional management curricula which presuppose there is a right way of managing). Rather than uncritically reproducing fixed representations of management, reflexive managers seek various conceptualizations and critiques of management as a means of exploring possibilities and rethinking what they would like organizations and management to be. And this is important given the pivotal role of organizations and managers in today's society.

▬▬ notes

1   See Argyris 1982; Lawler 1985; Schön 1983; Vaill 1989; and Whetton and Cameron 1983.
2   See Chia and Morgan, 1996; Ford and Harding 2007; French and Grey 1996; Ghoshal 2005; *Management Learning* Special Issue 2009; Parker 2002 and Willmott 1994.
3   See Chapter 2 in Hatch and Cunliffe (2006) for a more detailed discussion of the history of organization studies, and Chapters 1 and 2 in Grey (2009) for further discussion on the Classical, Scientific Management and Human Relations Schools.
4   See Drucker (1973) for a discussion of the history, challenges and tasks of a manager.
5   See http://www.escp-eap.eu/escp-eap/about-escp-eap/history-of-escp-eap-the-school-of-management-for-europe/.
6   See Pfeffer and Fong (2002) for a brief history.
7   For example, Hales 1986; Horne and Lupton 1965; Sayles 1964.
8   See also: Alvesson and Willmott, 1992, 1996; Grey and Willmott 2005; Harding 2003.
9   Terms coined respectively by George Ritzer (1995) and Sharon Zukin (1996).
10 Cited with permission.
11 *Encarta World English Dictionary.*
12 See the Kepner-Tregoe website http://www.kepner-tregoe.com/TheKTWay/Our Processes. cfm (accessed August 2008).
13 http://www.youtube.com/watch?v=ISiQA6KKyJo.
14 First published in Cunliffe (2001).
15 See http://www.citehr.com/11230-engaging-employees-through-leadership-story-telling-eds.html (accessed 28.8.08).
16 See Cunliffe, (2009) for further discussion.

2

Managing, Language and Communication
(Or 'That's not what I said...')

We must maintain that level of quality, so I manage by wandering around. I do, if you will, kind of feel the pulse of the airport. I talk to stakeholders – the carriers, I talk to the vendors, I talk to the passengers. If you're walking down the concourse and pass a cart I say, 'would you mind telling me, in just a minute here, what was your experience going through this airport? Going through security?' Passengers come up with some good suggestions sometimes. So all of those things mean I'm not going to be surprised. I try to get around. I think communication is critical.

When you get to an airport, you tend to be nervous, you're not sure what to do, you're not sure where to go. So we've picked out people that have shown this ability to communicate effectively and connect with people. They'll start talking to people, 'How are you ma'am? Where are you heading today? You know, you're in a long line, why don't you just sit down there ... Just check your bag right here and you're going to be okay...' You see the stress level go right down!

The Airport Director goes to Washington often ... he loves to talk about relationships, partnerships, and dealing with the way we've been able to solve problems.

(Excerpts from an interview with a Federal Security Director of a
US Airport)

Many problems in organizations are blamed on poor communication and misunderstandings. As the Federal Security Director says in the quote above, communication is critical – and communication is not just about talking to people, but connecting with people and establishing relationships. It's the latter that's often forgotten or ignored in the drive to discover how managers can communicate their ideas more effectively so that they can link the performance of employees to organizational goals. In this chapter I'd like to focus on the idea of managing as a relational practice and offer some ideas about language and the world that reveal a new landscape of possibilities for the way we communicate with each other, not only in management, but in every aspect of life. It's a way of thinking that grew out of a range of disciplines, including philosophy, anthropology, sociology and, in particular, linguistics – disciplines that explore the different ways in which we engage with our world. This might give you the impression that what follows will be an extremely abstract and obtuse examination of densely theoretical material. On the contrary, while it does involve examining some basic philosophical, sociological and linguistic premises, our discussion is about everyday talk and the crucial nature of language in the everyday life of any manager. This is based on the premise that every aspect of management involves language and some form of communication, and that being aware of how language works can enhance communication.

This chapter is about how we somehow manage to connect with each other and coordinate our actions in vaguely meaningful ways, and why it's important for managers to understand and explore some very different ideas about what it is that we might be doing when we are communicating with organizational members. The idea that our actions are only 'vaguely meaningful' might seem a particularly pessimistic view, but we know communication is not easy, and the vagaries were brought home to me a couple of years ago in a conversation with a US colleague who asked me (so I thought) how my daughter was. I said she was in the UK and not too happy. He asked if I'd 'had her flown out there' and what would I do if she 'had health problems'? He talked about how his 19-year-old died, and during the last year was so ill he didn't like to go on vacation and leave her with a sitter. Despite being perplexed by his turn of phrase, we continued talking for about 10 minutes – until we realized we were talking about two completely different things: he was talking about dogs and I was talking about my daughter!

No one would argue against the statement that communication is a crucial management skill, and any manager will tell you that she or he spends most of the day communicating with a wide variety of people, both within and outside the organization, on a range of issues including strategy, performance issues, financial reports, equipment breakdowns, and so on. Many will have studied communication as part of a management training and education programme. A quick internet search on management communication reveals a vast number of courses on communication skills, listening techniques, body language, presentation skills, assertiveness, and the list goes on. Most management and organizational behaviour textbooks have at least one chapter on the topic, which usually defines communication as an exchange of information with the goal of achieving mutual understanding, and presents a model of the communication process that looks something like Figure 3.

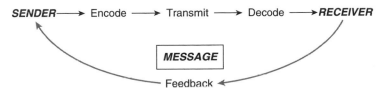

Figure 3   A model of the communication process

So, given that there's a lot of stuff out there on communication – forgive the play on words – but what more is there to say and what can be said that's any different? Is there anything that's not 'communication-as-usual' wrapped up differently?

I think there is. There's a different way of communicating that is not just another management technique, but involves a fundamentally different way of thinking about how language works and the nature of our relationships with other people: as the Director says in the quotes at the beginning of this chapter, of thinking about communication as relationships and connecting. This different way of thinking about communication means we will encounter a strange world, a different 'language', and unfamiliar and curious forms of seeing, saying and doing. But I ask you to be open-minded about what follows, because I believe these ideas are crucial for the notion of managing as a relational practice, and for the way managers interact with and manage people. Before we explore these ideas, let's unpack some taken-for-granted notions about communication – and this means that we need to address two main philosophical concerns and build on the ideas we discussed in Chapter 1: what is the nature of reality (*ontology*), and how do we understand and create knowledge about reality (*epistemology*)?

▬▬▬ unpacking 'communication'

Figure 3 is not *just* a model of the communication process. Whether we realize it or not, the model also holds a number of assumptions about the nature of reality and language (*ontology*), how we understand and make sense of reality and language (*epistemology*), and what ideal ways of communicating should look like. And the performative nature of language and of models and theories such as this, constitutes our way of communicating and relating to people. So what are these assumptions?

- First, that there is a *world out there* that exists separately from us, that we can all talk about and understand in the same way.
- That we can *represent* or accurately describe the world through language – as long as we use the correct language and get the communication process right.
- That a message contains words that mean some*thing*, they describe an object, an emotion, etc., and we all understand that meaning in the same way.
- That there are *independent and autonomous* senders and receivers, each with a message in mind that they want to convey to the other.
- The sender *first thinks* of what she or he wants to say and the best way of saying it (encodes) *before transmitting* the message.
- The receiver hears/reads the message and *decodes its real meaning*. If the receiver doesn't understand, for whatever reason, he or she will indicate this through feedback, which then enables the sender to rephrase the message or add further information. So communication is a recursive process culminating in an agreement over meaning.

These assumptions constitute what is known as a *realist* view of the world – that there is a real, independently existing reality. The consequences of this model for management communication are that managers need to learn to speak and write effectively because management is about the art of persuasion – of being able to use appropriate words and modes of transmission so that employees understand what you *really* mean, and being able to articulate a message in a persuasive way so they will actually do what you want them to do. The view of managers as rational agents is based on a realist perspective. As we will see later in this chapter and in Chapter 3, this understanding of language and communication also carries implicit assumptions about power that are enacted in our day-to-day relations with others. But for the moment let's focus on communication.

Is this how we actually communicate on a day-to-day basis? When we are talking to each other, do we deliberately and consciously formulate every sentence, or pause to decode what the other person is saying? Well yes, sometimes we might: if a manager is about to talk to an employee or a group of employees about the budget deficit or changes to the marketing strategy, then she is likely to sit down and think about what she's going to say. But unless she actually writes this down and reads it word for word, then what she says will be a mix of previously thought words and sentences, along with improvisations as she responds to the other person. And on a moment-to-moment basis we usually talk without any pauses in the conversation. In everyday conversations we respond to others in spontaneous and instinctive ways, and our conversations have an often unnoticed rhythm and flow, which gives us an overall sense and meaning. Let me give an example from a research conversation I had with a Programme Manager a few years ago. We were talking about some of the problems he dealt with on a day-to-day basis. Notice the rhythm of his words and how this supports what he's saying and reinforces an impression of the ambiguity of his job – an intuitive managing of meaning:

> Problems are at a much higher level of abstraction; nothing is designed, nothing is given, everything is what you decide it is. If you ask somebody, 'What is this product going to do?' 'Well I don't know, you tell me.' 'When is it going to be finished?' 'Well I don't know – you tell me.' 'How much is it going to cost?' 'Well I don't know – you tell me...'

This was part of a two-hour conversation, part of his normal way of talking and unrehearsed. Did he first think he would phrase his comment in this way and then say it? Listening to the audiotape, there was no pause before he spoke – he just continued to talk. Interestingly, French philosopher Merleau-Ponty says, 'I do not speak *of* my thoughts; I *speak them*, and what is between them – my after-thoughts and underthoughts' (1964: 19). The point he's making is that we don't necessarily think *then* speak – we speak *and* think and often speak *then* think. So thinking and speaking are not separate activities but are somehow entwined and complete each other. To reinforce this point, next time you are having a conversation, try fig-uring out when you are speaking and when you are thinking – it's not easy! In this way, as Merleau-Ponty (1962) argues, language outruns us because we say more than we think and, as we talk and respond to each other, multiple meanings emerge. This can create problems if we assume that there's only one meaning (mine), it's the right mean-ing, and that *you* just didn't understand what I was saying. This may explain why you often hear people say 'But that's not what I said!', 'Why don't you listen?', or 'That's not what I asked you to do!'

Before we explore communication and language further, I'd like to offer a different set of assumptions to the ones listed above. These assumptions offer a basis for examining a different way of thinking about how we communicate, interact and relate with others. I'm going to spend a bit more time discussing these assumptions because they really lay the foundation for the idea that managing is about how we relate to people and the world around us.

alternative ways of thinking about language, reality and communication ... and their impact on management

The main point of this chapter is that language is a crucial yet often taken-for-granted aspect of managing organizations, important because everything a manager does involves some form of language – implementing strategy, monitoring budgets, encouraging people to work together, communicating goals, and so on. However, we need to move away from traditional ways of thinking about language and the belief that communication is an orderly, structured process in which we just have to select the correct words to accurately describe whatever we are referring to. No, when we *live* language and communication, it's messier, fascinatingly complex, and our conversations are not wholly under our control. Yet, despite this, we somehow muddle through, we talk with other people and manage to get things done. But how?

Within the field of organization studies there lies a whole range of ideas about the nature and role of language in management: from the more conventional communication models as described in Figure 3 – where language straightforwardly describes what is out there, to the idea that language is all there is, that is, that there is nothing, or no *thing* outside language and that as humans we are just linguistic nodes, products of various discourses or ways of speaking (a somewhat bizarre idea when carried to extremes). Let's look at some alternative ways of thinking about reality and language and why these might be of interest to managers.

so what is 'reality'?

The world is wholly inside and I am wholly outside myself.

Merleau-Ponty, 1962: 474

What if we move away from the realist view of the world and begin with the idea that social realities are not separate from people? What if we see ourselves and our world as intimately interwoven because each shapes and is shaped by the other in everyday interactions and conversations? In other words, we *talk* what we understand as our social world into existence, and maintain 'its' existence in our talk, while at the same time what we believe is the outside social world, plays back into what we do and say. To employ an academic label – realities are performatively and *socially constructed*. We might think and talk of the social world and organizations as real and independent of whatever we say and do, but they take on a reality in our talk.

M.C. Escher's lithograph *Drawing Hands* (1948) aptly captures the paradoxical nature of this view of social reality. You may recall the lithograph is of two hands emerging from a sheet of paper, both holding pencils and drawing each other. Just as we ask how can two hands draw each other into existence – so we ask how we can shape a world that we think already exists? Merleau-Ponty discusses this at some length in the *Phenomenology of Perception* (1962). He argues that there isn't an objective world out there that we each perceive in the same way, but that we and the world are dialectically related. What does this mean?

Dialectics is usually associated with dualisms – the idea that there are two opposing terms or situations that are perceived as irreconcilable, and so one is often chosen over the other. In management this may relate to quantity versus quality, centralization versus decentralization, a short-term versus a long-term orientation, and so on. Merleau-Ponty finds dualisms problematic: the idea that there is a separate mind and body, body and soul, reason and emotion, thought and speech, a person and a world … This separation is known as Cartesian dualism, after the French philosopher René Descartes, who argued that mind and body are not the same and are in fact separate: the mind is intellectual, a consciousness without physical substance, whereas the body has substance – it takes up space but it doesn't think. Merleau-Ponty argued against these dualisms, suggesting that mind–body, person–world, you–I, and so on, are inseparable – are *dialectical*, which for Merleau-Ponty means two separate terms only becoming themselves through each other (for example, Escher's *Drawing Hands*). So this brings us to the idea that managing as relational practice is not just about relating to other people, but is about how we see our relationship between ourselves and the world around us.

For example, he suggests the human dialectic means that we create social (and organizational) structures and practices which exist in our interactions, but that we see as being independent from us and influencing, even determining, those actions. Consequently, these 'structures' can imprison us, they shape what we can and cannot do because we don't recognize we ourselves have created and maintained them in our actions and interactions. We don't necessarily see or understand this continually changing dialectical relationship and the part we play.

You might be raising your eyebrows rather cynically at this point … Where is this going and how does it relate to management? The person–world dualism has implications for how we view and manage organizations. For example, the idea of the rational manager is typical of Cartesian dualism: emotions (the body) should not interfere with the rational working of the mind, because emotion is irrational and impacts our ability to be objective. Yet, as we've seen, there's more than one rationality, and what is objective to me might seem completely arbitrary to you. Let's begin to explore the dialectical nature of social reality.

The idea of a socially constructed world gained attention with Berger and Luckmann's influential book *The Social Construction of Reality*, in which they proposed that society exists as both an objective and subjective reality. As they rather paradoxically stated: 'Society is a human product. Society is an objective reality. Man is a social product' (1966: 61). They argued that the social world is humanly produced in ongoing activity and routines, yet we experience it as being objective because it both affects our lives on an ongoing basis and we have to go out and learn about it.

Let's look at this in management and organizational terms. Organizations don't exist by themselves, but in the interactions and conversations and activities of organizational members. That's not to say that there aren't physical aspects of organizations – of course there are buildings, machines, desks and products. But what gives the organization its identity and managers their authority? How do people do their work and coordinate their actions, and how do products and services come into being? Formal policies, operating procedures and job descriptions have some sort of 'thingness' because they are words on paper – but they exist and take on meaning as people talk and act in relation to them. Job descriptions, for example, are maintained through our everyday activities, through common ways of talking and through routine behaviours and interactions. Job descriptions don't *do* things by themselves. So it's a bit of a cop out when organizational members say they can't change things or deal with problems effectively because 'it's the system'. What is *the system*, who creates it, and who keeps it going? We talk and act 'systems' into being, and maintain their existence in our talk 'about' them. This requires a shift in thinking, because it means seeing the world in social interactions and relationships rather than in structures and systems. And while cultural anthropologists and sociologists such as Clifford Geertz (1983), James Clifford (1983) and George Marcus (with Fischer, 1986) have long questioned our relationship with our social world and the ways in which we account for our experience, the majority of research in management and organization studies still takes a realist perspective by studying organization structures and systems, management roles, and identifying the laws, principles and norms that influence human behaviour. However, these laws and principles are constructed by academics to explain our world – so do such laws *really* exist?

Berger and Luckmann's main premise, that social realities and identities are created and maintained in conversations and social interactions rather than in structures, has been taken up by scholars in a number of disciplines, who have developed the notion that social reality, identities and knowledge are culturally, socially, historically and linguistically influenced. Language does not describe the world, it *is* the world because it shapes how we see, act and experience our world. For Merleau-Ponty speech is originary and creative because it's how we talk things into being – just as a painter begins with a blank canvas and uses colour, form and space to create a work of art, so we create meaning and our experience of our world as we speak. And meaning is more than words, for just as a painting can evoke a range of emotions, so can our words – both may open up new ways of seeing, saying and acting: new possibilities for relating with others. We think, talk, argue, write, remember, love, manage and control others in language. In *other words*, we cannot separate language, ourselves and the world: they exist in a mutual relationship. As Michael Agar says in *Language Shock*, 'They're wrapped up together like hydrogen and oxygen in water. You can't pull them apart and still have the water to drink' (1994: 66). We saw in Chapter 1 how this idea helps construct management in different ways, through the idea of managers as storytellers, managers of meaning, practical authors, and reflexive practitioners. And we'll explore what this means for managing organizations in Chapter 3. What I'd like to do now is focus on language and the relational nature of managing.

how does language work?

So this brings us to our next main premise – that language doesn't represent the world, it *is* our world. Indeed, as Bakhtin says, 'All the diverse areas of human activity involve the use of language' (1986: 60). Okay, let's say you buy in, at least a little bit, to this idea that we shape our social realities through language – then what is language, how does it work, and why do managers need to think about language? If language doesn't describe things, then what does it do and how does it shape our world? This is where we are going to get into some pretty complex ideas about the nature of language, but I want to ground these as much as possible in practical examples from managers, because this is the point – language *is* our experience.

I'd like to go back to the research I did for my Ph.D., because this was when the importance of language first struck me. One of my research sites was a small US manufacturing organization. I had an initial conversation with the President of the company before talking to the senior managers, spending time in the organization, and talking to first line supervisors on workshops. In our initial taped conversation, the President commented:

> I live in this world of uncertainty. I am not naive any longer – I come in in the morning now and I'm a sceptic. I say, 'Okay, first tell me about all the casualties, I want to set priorities. What are the things that might take us out of business today?' I'm not being wise, I'm being a realist … Right now we're wrestling with keeping two boilers up and running …

I didn't really think about the language he used until listening to tapes of my conversations with other members of the organization. It was then I began to realize that there seemed to be a common way of speaking about the organization that gave me a sense of the organization as a battlefield. Indeed the President had used this term on a number of occasions. The battlefield metaphor played through my conversations with other managers and employees who used words like 'shotgun approaches', 'keep them in our camp', 'stay on your toes', 'run up the red flag'. Such metaphors can be very powerful in shaping the ways in which people talk, think and act, because a shared common sense emerges about the nature of organizational life. If a senior manager comes in every day and asks about 'casualties', he or she will be told what all the problems are. Pretty soon this will be part of everyday ways of talking in the organization. And organizational members will see this as what the organization is *really* like – which will continue to influence their ways of talking and acting … Precisely the *Drawing Hands* paradox and Merleau-Ponty's human dialectic!

What's interesting is that this is usually not obvious to organizational members. I had a final meeting with the President when I showed him a transcript of our conversations and asked him about his comments. He was shocked, he hadn't realized he was using this language, nor had he thought about its impact. He asked what he could do? What about if he came in every morning and asked what was going well and what could be built upon and improved? How might that influence the way people talked about and perceived the organization?

I've cited the conversation with the President and other managers before, because they are wonderful examples of the powerful, sedulous and sometimes insidious nature of language (Cunliffe, 2001, 2002a, 2002b). Yes, managers think about how to phrase mission and vision statements, or what words to use in formal statements and written documents – but they don't always think about what they say in conversations, or about the powerful nature of everyday ways of speaking. The example above illustrates a point made by Merleau-Ponty that 'Speech is, therefore, that paradoxical operation through which, by using words of a given sense, and already available meanings, we try to follow up an intention which necessarily outstrips, modifies, and in itself, in the last analysis, stabilizes the meanings of the words which translate it' (1962: 452). In other words, the President was using familiar words, but by his use of these particular words in this context, and the way others understood and responded to his use of these words, stable meanings and ways of acting emerged that he did not necessarily intend. And all this was not a conscious process, nor was it under any one person's control, it happened over time and in many conversations. Did he intend to convey a sense of the organization as a chaotic battlefield? No, but this is what emerged – his words outstripped him! And this goes on every day in all organizations, in conversations about strategy, about the provision of services, market brand, improving customer service ... You can begin to understand the crucial influence of everyday ways of talking by looking at how organizational members talk: the words, phrases, metaphors they use and how these relate to the way things are done. Language works in subtle ways, which is why managers need to move beyond the conventional model of communication to understand the power of their words.

You might be getting the idea that the world is *only* about language, or that anything goes – that we can say and therefore create absolutely anything. There are some scholars, mainly poststructuralists, who think language is all there is, and we will look at this work later. But for the moment let's begin with some less radical ideas about the nature of language and how it works.

Linguists study language. The father of modern linguistics is Ferdinand de Saussure, a Swiss linguist whose teachings were compiled by his students in the 1959 book *Course in General Linguistics* (first published in 1911). Saussure wished to study language scientifically, to describe how language existed at particular points in time. But he realized that he could not study speech itself (*la parole*), because the spoken word is too idiosyncratic, too full of hesitations and reformulations. Yet, at any one moment in time, people have knowledge of grammatical forms of talk as a result of their shared use of language (*la langue*). So he felt our *knowledge of language* is very orderly and could be studied in a systematic manner. When we are presented with various sentences and asked to judge whether they are grammatically correct or not, we can do so. We know which words are 'proper' and which are not, and we know how words have to be used in particular ways in a sentence. Remember English grammar at school and the exercise of mapping sentence structures? This is known as *prescriptive* linguistics because it's concerned with how we *should* speak – and while prescriptive linguistics might define what is acceptable, our everyday use of language is not that precise! You might remember one of the famous catchphrases of British comedians Eric Morecambe and Ernie Wise, 'The play what I wrote'. There's no way this can be seen as the correct way of talking, but it was a way of talking that Morecambe and Wise drew upon precisely because its very unacceptability made a humorous point in that particular dramatic context (that ostensibly Ernie thought his rather ambitious, badly written and trite plays were really good!), and the phrase made its way into everyday conversation at that time.

So not only is language fascinatingly complex, it's also very clever, and we understand this intuitively and engage in its multifariousness on a day-to-day basis! A number of organizational scholars have studied this aspect of language in an organizational context. Mary Jo Hatch (1997) studied how a team of managers engaged in irony as a means of understanding and dealing with the complexities of organizational life.

She suggested that irony offers a way of grappling with possibilities and impossibilities because of its contradictory nature, and because it engages humour and emotion that can lend a sense of sharing – of being in this together – that might otherwise be difficult to create. This shared meaning is not explicitly agreed, it just happens, and it has an impact on the way we feel about the organization or situation. One organization I worked for years ago was experiencing a leadership crisis, and a colleague made the comment, 'All we need now is for X to step up to the plate!' Of course, this was the last thing we wanted because X would cause even more havoc and conflict, but the ensuing laughter relieved tension and, as Hatch suggests, allowed new constructions of the future to take place in a less threatening atmosphere. Bakhtin argues that irony is a way of rising above a situation and that 'Only dogmatic and authoritarian cultures are one-sidedly serious' (1986: 134). So managers need to be aware that it's not just formal and prescriptive language that shapes meaning – but that informal everyday ways of talking can have much more of an impact than they might imagine! And their everyday talk impacts relationships and how organizational members relate to each other.

Saussure also described language as a system of *signs*, letters and words that we string together in particular ways to make sentences that mean something. Signs consist of *signifiers* (the shape and sound of a word, e.g. t-a-b-l-e) and *signifieds* (the object or concept that the signifier is about), and it's when the signifiers and signified come together that the sign takes on some kind of meaning. If you hear someone say the word 'table' (the signifier), you have an idea of what that actually means – a square wooden object with four legs (the signified). But as we have seen, language isn't that simple! When hearing 'table', you might think of a round glass table with a central marble stand, a stainless steel writing table, a small rectangular coffee table…, and so the relationship between signifiers and signified can be *arbitrary* because signifiers have a number of different meanings. I can of course be more specific and say 'Last night I went to dinner with three friends and we sat around a wonderful small oval antique wooden table with…', but this is still open to interpretation (how small, what type of wood and so on). However, the example does bring us to another point Saussure made – that it's the *relationship between signs in a sentence* that helps create meaning, not the words themselves. We use the same words in many different contexts in which the meaning varies – 'I'll *tell* you what to do', 'I couldn't *tell* them apart', 'I'm going to *tell* on you', 'It was a *tell-all* book.' In these examples, *tell* variously means inform, distinguish, report, reveal. It's the context in which the words are used, the sentence and the situation, that give words and signs meaning. Saussure believed this is why we needed to develop a language system to explain how signs are organized into meaning and how language works.

Not only are there many possible meanings of signifiers, but things become more arbitrary at times when the signifier and signified don't connect. This was made patently clear to me during a five-hour bus trip through Mexico to visit a friend. I spoke no Spanish, and no one on the bus spoke English. I could hear the signifiers (the words) but had no clue what they meant. I coped with the few stops in the journey by watching everyone else, tagging along at the back, and making sure I didn't wander too far from the bus because I'd no idea what time it would leave. My inability to combine signifiers and signified into meaningful signs became more problematic at the end of the trip. I'd expected to arrive at a bus station where I would meet my friend, but the driver dropped people off at their houses and obviously wanted to do the same for me. We gave up trying to communicate, and, thankfully, he drove to the bus garage where I found somebody who spoke a little English and phoned my friend. This example illustrates another key aspect of Saussure's work – that meaning emerges in language use or in actual speech (*parole*): signs and social life are intimately connected, and language use is culture and community specific. This has implications for managing because it implies that written words (e.g., vision and mission statements) are not enough, we talk through and create shared meanings about goals, strategy and values, etc., in our everyday conversations. We can also identify particular forms of discourse in organizations, which often don't make sense to new employees or to people outside the organization such as customers, patients, suppliers, etc.

And we are not just talking about different languages. When I first moved from the UK to the US, I discovered the normal response to 'Hi, how are you?' was not the typically British 'Oh, not too bad', because this caused the inquirer to stop in their tracks. A perky 'Fine, how are you?!' was expected. It actually took me a number of years to manage this reply because the other was so deeply ingrained and habitual. I was equally astounded that US managers often used the phrase 'No problem' in response to requests to do something, without seeming to assess first whether it would be a problem or not. I was more familiar with UK manager responses which were usually more tentative in nature. Of course misunderstandings arise when we have to work in different cultures without realizing that different linguistic conventions and embedded ways of talking exist, and that they are performative because we begin to make judgements that affect how we interact with people. For example, the perception that US managers are brash and want to do things now, so don't consult them until we've considered all our options, versus UK managers, who never give you a straight answer and play for time, so it's better just to get the job done yourself. Okay, while these might be (not entirely unfamiliar) extremes, my point is that it's important for managers to be reflexively aware of different ways of talking and the impact on everyday interaction. This requires paying attention not only to what we say, but also to what we assume, and one of the main assumptions we need to question is that we all understand things in the same way.

managing as relational practice: language, real conversations and real people

I've tried to emphasize the role that language plays in everything we do, and want to go on to explore in more depth why this is crucial to managing people and organizations. This is also where we'll expand on the idea of managing as relational practice: that whatever managers do, it is not in isolation, but always in relation to other people, communities and ways of talking.

Saussure's ideas were taken up, developed and challenged by other linguists across a range of disciplines including psychology, sociology and organization studies. While his work was incredibly influential in drawing attention to language use and the idea that speech is creative, unique and individual, he was more concerned with identifying general language systems. It was this interest that led to the development of *semiotics,* an emerging field in organization studies with particular relevance for understanding organization culture. We will explore semiotics further in Chapter 3. But it was Mikhail Mikhailovich

Bakhtin, a Russian literary theorist, who took up what Saussure had thought too complex to study: speech and the act of speaking itself. Bakhtin found the notion of linguistic systems and linguistic analysis problematic, because they focused on 'the relationships among elements within the language system' (1986: 118) and ignored real conversations, real people and the responsive nature of understanding and meaning. I'd like to pick up three aspects of his work because they have particular relevance for the ways in which we manage people and organizations: dialogism, speech genres, and heteroglossia.

Bakhtin wasn't concerned with developing a model of communication (as in Figure 3) – but rather with exploring ways of thinking about language and *living speech*, that is, how we actually speak to each other (Saussure's *la parole*), in all its living detail. You rarely come across Bakhtin's work in management literature and on management courses, which is a pity because he offers a number of insights into how we live our lives with others. And one theme that particularly fascinates me that runs throughout his work, is his idea that we are always in relation to an 'other': another particular person, a context, a way of speaking and a culture. This means that we do not have complete freedom or control in what we say and, I suggest, means that *we therefore have a responsibility to consider 'others' as we speak*.

Let's begin with dialogism. Bakhtin (1986) differentiated between monologic and dialogic language. Think of a monologue in a play – a speech by one actor to other actors or to the audience – which captures a number of elements of Bakhtin's monologism: a single *author*ity who is unresponsive to how his or her voice is being received, a particular view or ideology, and an aim of coming to a common understanding of a pre-established view. We typically think of this way of relating as autocratic management. Bakhtin criticized the oppressive nature of monologic discourse, suggesting that it rules out diverse meanings and silences other voices. He argued that we need to focus on the *dialogic* aspect of language as living utterances – the two-way movement of dialogue between people in particular moments and particular settings. Dialogism takes into account 'others' because it means recognizing that meaning emerges in the 'interaction and struggle' (1986: 92) of back and forth conversation between people. This struggle occurs in the specific moments of conversation, but these moments also occur within a general context of wider meanings. He explained this relationship by suggesting that our conversations consist of a person who speaks, a person who listens (the addressee), and a *superaddressee*, an invisible third agency that exists outside the conversation. The superaddressee is not necessarily another person, but is rather a need to be understood by others beyond the immediate conversation; by a person, a group of people, a community, and so on – to whom or to which we must be *responsive* and *responsible* in our talk. What we say both has meanings unique to the context in which we speak, and carries with it broader meanings that need to be understood by others who may not be present at the time of speaking. So when a group of senior managers are engaged in discussion about, let's say, business strategy or market brand, they need to consider not only the other listeners in the room, but be responsive to the needs and understandings of the superaddressee (shareholders, customers, the local community, the media, etc.). Dialogism means being open to others, to various voices and meanings, and to the need for dialogue and discussion as integral to responsive and ethical management. Thus *dialogism is about relating to others.*

Monologic and dialogic ways of talking therefore have implications for managing organizations because much of the official and formal communication that goes on in organizations is of a monologic form. Mission, vision and value statements are designed to create a single unified meaning and to direct the behaviour of employees. Courses on management communication often incorporate techniques such as framing and impression management – ways not only of presenting information but also of presenting ourselves to others in order to influence their perceptions of us in a favourable way. According to Fairhurst and Sarr (1996) framing is an essential leadership skill involving the use of language to shape the way in which people interpret and give meaning to situations, and this is crucial because meaning influences action. Impression management is also about shaping meaning in a wider sense; not just through language but also through how we present ourselves and our organizations in order to construct a desirable social identity (Kakabadse, Bank and Vinnicombe, 2004) and a positive organization identity (Schultz, Hatch and Larsen, 2002). These are monologic forms of communication because they aim to impose a particular meaning on others. However they often fail in this aim, because different people *interpret* differently what is said, what is written and how we act. We will explore the implications of monologism for managing organizations further in Chapter 3. Meanwhile, consider the potentially misleading, insincere and manipulative nature of such forms of monologic discourse, and how people respond to this. And consider how much of the conversation that goes on in organizations is monologic or is genuinely dialogic.

Bakhtin (1986) also suggested that all human activity involves language, and that language consists of relatively stable ways of speaking used in particular contexts. These stable ways of speaking become obvious when you move into new or different contexts. As a manager you will find yourself using 'management' language (bottom line, deliverables, metrics). As a student of management at university and college, you probably find yourself having to talk about mimetic isomorphism, LMX theory and poststructuralism. My point is that there are different ways of speaking, or as Bakhtin says, *speech genres*, that occur in different contexts; business, technical, scientific, academic, legal, etc. Speech genres consist of primary genres – the simple, unmediated utterances of everyday conversation, and secondary speech genres – the complex, organized, ideological, premeditated forms of communication we find in scientific research, novels, and formal organization documents and statements. Bakhtin believed that if we focus on secondary speech genres alone, we lose our immediate relation to reality because secondary genres reduce complex and ever-changing experience to a particular logic, category or theoretical forms of talk. A profit and loss account, a company annual report, an organization's strategy document, are all examples of secondary speech genres that can and do simplify and mask the challenges and complexities of everyday organizational life. Have you ever sat in class listening to someone talk about planning techniques, strategic analysis, or six principles for building and motivating teams, and thought – if only life was that simple?!

So what does this mean for managers and managing organizations? In *In Search of Management* (2001), Tony Watson talks about two competing languages in the organization he studied. One, an official language represented in formal documents (monologic, secondary speech genres) was about empowerment and growth, the other was the unofficial or 'actual' language – how managers spoke to each other on a day-to-day basis (dialogic, primary speech genres), and was about the pressure to control costs and jobs. He found that while some managers operated in either the official or the unofficial language, others switched confusingly between the two. Part of the official language involved talking about 'skill grades' instead of 'jobs', but Watson found there was resistance to this monologic 'language reform' by managers continuing to use the 'illegal language' (p. 115). Dialogic and monologic ways of talking, primary and secondary speech genres play through and influence our ways of talking, often without us realizing it – which takes us back to the idea that language does things in specific moments but also works beyond us. So it's important to think about how we relate to others: the day-to-day impact of what we say (and write), about what meanings we impose, who we exclude, who we allow to speak, and how people respond.

The notion of speech genres also highlights the notion that making sense of what's going on around us is not just an intellectual activity taking place inside our heads using theory and models, but it is a practical, relational, responsive activity occurring in our everyday conversations. So reading a book about management techniques, or having a policy document or mission statement (both secondary speech genres) only goes so far – it's what we do and say (primary speech genres) that counts. It's in our living dialogic relationships, our relationally responsive interaction, that we create meanings, make sense of what's happening around us, and work out what needs to be done (Cunliffe, 2008; Shotter and Cunliffe, 2002).

Let me give an example from my own research. We typically think of research interviews (structured or unstructured) as involving carefully worded questions, that is, as a monologic and secondary speech genre. But the answers to our questions are unscripted and we often find ourselves working out meaning with our research 'subjects' depending on the dialogic overtones and nuances of our utterances, that is, as a primary speech genre. Notice in the excerpt below from one of my research conversations how Paul and I respond to each other:

PAUL: I was just recently approached by the EDA, saying would I mind joining the Board of Directors? ... These are the sorts of things ... ummm ... I have to start positioning myself and it creates a little anxiety because it's like, you know, I'll be leaving the store – is it okay? Is the support there? Is the organization up to the level it should be?

ANN: So the anxiety is about what you're leaving, not what you're going to?

PAUL: Yes. I'll be honest with you, a morning like today, I've enjoyed because it's stimulating, and I've done this with the managers, when you pull them away. We go to [offsite] – you've been there – or somewhere, and you talk about the business objectives. It allows you to kind of assess, look forward, and when you're there it's almost like unreal ... you know [at work] you're in a meeting and phones are ringing and there's someone in the office and you ... Well, you'll see – we can't be accused of high overheads! [*Laughs*] We're on one another's shoulders, worrying about what's in ...

ANN: So on site it's easy to be managed by the detail?

PAUL: Yes ... we've no closed doors. But when I really have something I want to sit down and focus on ... right now we need to understand our competitors, one of whom has been taken over by the Japanese, which may mean we have to become more aggressive.

ANN: Will this have a big impact on the business?

PAUL: There'll be further decline – even if it's 5 per cent but it's only going to go so far, there'll always be a need for the product. I don't know if we want to position ourselves as the buggy whip in manufacturing but we'll survive, and we'll have the best organization in place, and no one else is around at our price.

This excerpt illustrates the relationally responsive nature of dialogue and the importance of speech genres in making sense. To use Bakhtin's terms, Paul and I are actively responsive to each other's comments, and not only does Paul explain in response to my questions, but he tries to orient me ('a morning like today', 'you've been there'), builds on utterances ('you know, you're in a meeting ...'), and anticipates ('Well, you'll see ...'). In this way, I'm an *active other* throughout the conversation, even though I may not be speaking at that moment. Paul draws on both primary ('phones are ringing') and secondary ('business objectives', 'overheads') speech genres. I later drew on academic speech genres relating to my research interests (as I am right now) to anticipate how I might write up the research. This excerpt also illustrates what Bakhtin calls the *expressive* aspect of dialogue – our emotional and evaluative connections to what (and to whom) we are talking. Contrary to the archetype of the rational manager who stands back and assesses situations objectively, whether we are conscious of it or not, every statement – its content and its style of utterance – is expressive. As Bakhtin says 'There can be no such thing as an absolutely neutral utterance' (1986: 84). Would Paul have exactly the same conversation, use the same words and say them in the same way to a different person? I doubt it. So the rational and the relationally responsive manager are two very different beings, and the relational view of managing goes beyond managers as storytellers and managers of meaning because while the latter imply some individual control over meaning, managing in a relational way accepts that meanings are shaped between people in conversations and shift with conversations. Relational managers therefore focus on dialogue (talking with) rather than monologue (talking to).

So how does relationally responsive dialogue differ from the communication model (Figure 3) we began with? This approach to language and communication is based on a different set of ontological assumptions: conversations are not about what exists and about finding the right words to convey the correct meaning – but about shaping meanings, understandings, and social realities *between us as we talk and respond to each other*. It's not about imposing meaning on others (monologue) but about dialogue, responsiveness and movement. Meaning does not lie in the words themselves, but in how we use words and put them together in a particular conversation – a conversation in which no one person has control because each is responding to the other with a superaddressee in mind. And such meaning is never finalized as something objective, but shifts within and across conversations. So rather than focus on an external model of communication, it's important for managers to think about how they actually talk and relate to people on a moment-to-moment basis. How might what I say, how I say it, and how I interact with someone influence his or her response and the meanings and understandings emerging between us? This is not a prescriptive approach to communication, it does not involve defining and using a language system, but it is *a reflexive and responsive approach*. It means being more careful and thoughtful about our everyday conversations because we recognize that we are (dialectically) shaping ever-changing and unfinished meanings and 'realities' in our dialogue.

Which brings us to the third point I wish to draw from Bakhtin's work (1981): that language is *heteroglossic*. Heteroglossia, literally *multispeechedness*, suggests that language is a complex mix of differences: between everyday speech and language systems, between primary and secondary speech genres, unofficial and official languages, national and local ways of talking, different styles, intonations, expressions, social and historically based ways of talking, and different worldviews or ideologies. These differences work both to unify (centripetal forces) and to resist or pull apart (centrifugal forces) meaning. Remember Tony Watson's example of the two languages? Both the official and unofficial language exemplified centripetal and centrifugal forces. While the unofficial language resisted the official it also unified the unofficial, it destabilized, polarized and unified talk. And while managers who are storytellers and managers of meaning often use language in a centripetal sense – to unify meaning and values and action – they also need to recognize the centrifugal forces leading to different versions of the story and different meanings. For example, a manager's heroic story about everyone pulling together to get the work done designed to motivate staff, can be treated with disdain by those staff who interpret it as a weak attempt to control and manipulate them.

To illustrate heteroglossia within everyday conversations, I'd like to take as an example, an imaginary project planning meeting between a department manager (DM) and her or his member of staff (MS). The dialogue might go along the lines of:

DM: Look, the bottom line is that these are the deliverables that have to be met. We have to create a product spec and product development process by June because they need to be incorporated in the operations manual. Production needs the specs to re-tool and start scheduling material deliveries. We agreed this a month ago.

MS: Yes, but Engineering haven't come up with the technical specs yet, and until they do we can't work on the product specs. I talked to one of the engineers, Dave, who told me he can't do anything as Phil [the Engineering Manager] told him to hold off ... I talked to Phil and *he* just came up with a list of reasons why they can't get the specs to us by the end of the month.

DM: It's his job! They held up the last project because they refused to accept our authority. He has to accept that's the authority structure.

MS: I think part of Phil's reluctance is that we've not been communicating the complexity of the project, so he doesn't understand the cost when they kick up a fuss for a week. I talked to R&D yesterday to get their input, and they are perfectly willing to help, but they want to be involved in planning discussions like these. If other departments were involved and part of the planning process they would feel taken care of and there'd be more buy-in ...

DM: It's not my job to mollycoddle people. I'll get on to Engineering and tell them we need the information by the end of the week ... I'm ultimately responsible for this project. Engineering just want their little fiefdom and need to realize my tolerance for stalling is low. They need to get moving.

There's a failure to understand the heteroglossic nature of dialogue on the part of DM, who assumes that everyone should see the situation the same way, and wants his/her voice to predominate. MS is far more attuned to heteroglossia: the different voices, meanings ('taken care of' versus 'mollycoddling'), ideas and speech types, and to the need to work towards the active understanding of the other (the Engineering Manager). Crucially, for Bakhtin, communication means dialogue – speaking *with* others in which all participate as equals, rather than rhetoric – speaking *to* others to persuade them.

Let's summarize these complex ideas and the implications for managing as a relational practice. First, words (signs) have various meanings that differ for different people in different contexts. Second, it's in our relationally responsive everyday conversations that we work out meanings, which dialectically shape and are shaped by our social, organizational and everyday experiences. Managers therefore need to pay attention to everyday ways of talking which are heteroglossic: carrying many different speech genres and different ways of talking that serve to both unify and disunify. Medvedev and Bakhtin talk about *speech tact* playing through every conversation, which is a rather nice way of thinking about these issues. Tact is not just politeness but being attuned to 'the social relationships of the speakers, their ideological horizons, and, finally, the concrete situation of the conversation' (1978: 95). But what does this actually mean in practice and why is this way of thinking about language and communication important? It means that we need to view communication as shaping meaning *together* as we speak. It means paying much more attention to 'others' in our everyday conversations: what we say, the words we use, how we speak, how people may respond to us and how we respond to them. It means questioning how monologic forms of talk and secondary speech genres may exclude others and limit our choices. And it means that managers need to think about what they do as always in relation to other people, and to carefully consider what they want that relationship to be.

language, différance and deconstruction

I mentioned earlier in the chapter that among the many different views of language, poststructuralists take the arbitrariness of signs and the questioning of single meanings even further than Saussure. Poststructuralism is both complex and philosophically dense, and I'm going to be pretty stark here and introduce some basic ideas that relate to the theme of language and management. While the connecting thread between social constructionism and poststructuralism is the belief that language shapes our realities, poststructuralists differ on how this occurs and on the role that we play as humans in the process. They take the 'social' and 'human' out of the process of construction and replace it with 'linguistic' and 'discourse'. Many poststructuralists using a Foucauldian perspective argue that realities are constructed by discursive practices (linguistic systems and ways of talking, texts, ways of thinking, etc.) and non-discursive practices (institutional structures, social practices, techniques, etc.) that regulate what is seen as 'normal'. Knowledge plays a disciplining role in this process because it consists of unconscious rules and practices that determine: what is 'good' knowledge; what are 'good' standards for judgement; who are experts, and therefore who can control meaning and speak for others. These practices are riddled with power, because they privilege particular ideologies, social structures, institutional practices and groups over others (Foucault, 1970, 1972). Poststructuralists are therefore interested in how language and language systems shape realities and identities – realities and identities (recall managers as discursive subjectivities) which are image-driven and image-inary, contradictory, fragmented and power-ridden. Before explaining how this relates to management, it's helpful to explain poststructuralist views of language.

For poststructuralists, meaning is not only arbitrary, but is always elusive. Derrida (1978) explained this through the notion of *différance*, which is a play on the French verb *différer*, meaning to differ and to defer. Recall from Chapter 1, his idea that words derive their meaning from their opposite (*differ*). Derrida also argued that meaning is always *defer*red, because in explaining the meaning of one word, you replace it with other words that are explained by yet other words, and so on. So if we look up the word 'manage' in the dictionary, we get a list of words, and we look up the meaning of these words …

> manage → organize → arrange → agree → consent →
> same opinion → view…

Thus *différance* is unending, because as you speak or write, you move further and further away from the original word or object you are attempting to describe. In contrast to Saussure, he argued that language has no fixed meaning because there is no direct link between signifiers and signifieds – we just have a chain of signifiers. The point is that meaning becomes ever more distant from its supposed starting point as it travels across time and space, so there is no original meaning. Turning this idea back on the statement I've just written, poststructuralists would say that there is no point – the point can never be fixed!

This idea of turning the idea back on itself raises another aspect of Derrida's work – that of *deconstruction*. Deconstruction is a way of reading texts to expose their multiple interpretations by different readers. This not only reveals the instability of meaning, but also the idea that once an author writes a text, she has no control over its meaning or the way in which readers might interpret it. In this way, readers are just as much authors of texts as authors! Derrida also argued that we need to deconstruct a text, not to find an alternative meaning, but to reveal its assumptions, contradictions and how the text might privilege one truth or position over another.

Joanne Martin (1990) brought deconstruction into the realm of organization studies when she deconstructed a story told by the CEO of a multinational corporation to illustrate the company's concern for women. The story was about a female employee who arranged her Caesarean section around the launch of a new product she had been involved in developing. The company provided a closed-circuit television by her bed so she could watch the launch event. Martin provided alternative readings, one of which reframed the story as a male employee, in the same situation, undergoing heart by-pass surgery. She argued that in both cases, the action illustrated a breach of the public (work) and private (personal life) divide, but in counterposing the two stories, the Caesarean example illustrated not a humanistic concern for the well-being of women, but a desire to maintain work productivity.

While deconstruction might seem like an academic, and (deliberately!) pointless linguistic exercise, I think it is important to managers because deconstructing organizational texts such as policy documents, mission and media statements, and even everyday emails, can sensitize us to hidden assumptions, silenced voices, to who or what is privileged, to alternative interpretations, and to consequences for organizational practices – intended or otherwise. Deconstruction can also help us raise a most critical question for managers: *Could what seems to me to be the 'reality' of the present situation be otherwise? Are there unnoticed openings for new possibilities and for taking a new direction?*

so is management all about language?

I started this chapter suggesting that language and communication are incredibly important to managers, but that traditional models can be problematic because they are based on specific assumptions that offer a particular view of the world that may be a limited, and possibly manipulative one. We then looked at some different ideas about the nature of language and its relationship to social reality that carry a very different way of looking at communication. From a social constructionist perspective, language both shapes and is shaped by our social and organizational realities. Language is also complex because meanings are arbitrary – depending on the moment and context in which we speak, listen, write and read. While meanings differ in each moment of speaking, there are particular ways of talking (secondary speech genres) that influence what we say. Speech is expressive and relationally responsive, and therefore never under the control of one person. We therefore need to be aware of the subtle and powerful ways in which language influences our lives: of its limiting and enlightening consequences. We will explore some of these consequences in the following chapter. For the moment I suggest that language isn't all there is – we live, feel, act, laugh, but we cannot escape its clutches because our acts and emotions take on meaning in language and help us connect with others. When we hear someone say 'I am angry' or 'I love you', we have a sense of what the person is feeling, even though 'anger' and 'love' might be expressed and felt differently. So let's be optimistic – language doesn't imprison us and determine everything we do or say. Rather it's a 'familiar room', carrying 'with it patterns of seeing, knowing, talking, and acting' (Agar, 1994: 71) that both shape what we say, do and who we are, and also offer possibilities for change.

3

Managing Hearts, Minds and Souls Or ... Obversion, Subversion and Diversion

If you pick up a book on management, organization theory or organizational behaviour, there's a good chance it will include something about organizational culture: the values, practices, stories, heroes and management style of an organization. Originally the purview of anthropologists who went out into the field to study the beliefs, customs and ways of living of indigenous populations, culture became big business in Organization Studies in the 1980s. Just as anthropologists lived in distant primitive societies to study their customs and traditions, organizational ethnographers began studying culture by spending time in organizations observing meetings and talking to employees to identify common assumptions, values and practices that influence organizational performance. Why is culture important? Because managing culture is about managing an organization's image with external and internal stakeholders, aligning individual goals with organizational goals, individual actions and identities with organizational requirements, and managing and motivating people. It's also, as we will see, about power and control: about managing identities and the hearts, minds, bodies and souls of people.

Edgar Schein's work has been influential in academic circles. His 1985 model of the three levels of organizational culture – with *assumptions* at the taken-for-granted and deepest level, *values* at the next and more accessible level, and finally *artifacts* at the most visible level – has formed the basis for many studies of organizational culture. But one of the precipitating factors in connecting academic with practitioner interest in culture was the advent of Tom Peters and Robert Waterman's 1982 book, *In Search of Excellence*, which identified the cultural attributes of successful organizations. Many books (both academic and popular press), TV programmes, videos, and countless seminars and televised national and worldwide conferences followed, in the almost evangelical fervour to reproduce cultures of 'excellence'. In academic terms this is known as *mimetic isomorphism* – modelling organizational practices, values and behaviours. Managers wanted to know how to create high performing companies through committed and highly motivated employees. The 1980s and 1990s saw the advent of mission and vision statements, the identification of core values (service excellence, quality, etc.), buzzwords such as empowerment and autonomy, catchy phrases ('There's no "I" in "Team"'; 'Go for the Low-hanging Fruit'), and images such as the Nike logo. These cultural texts and artifacts are connected with the idea of managers as actors and managers of meaning, defining reality by managing front stage performances, creating heroic images, symbols and stories, framing language and speaking rhetorically to powerfully manage the hearts, minds and emotions of employees. Culture management is a key element of the managerialization and professionalization of management ... and is also open to destabilization and critique.

In his ethnographic study of culture in a US engineering company, Gideon Kunda found that 'management pays a great deal of attention to developing, articulating, and disseminating the organizational ideology for internal consumption' (1992: 218). Senior managers 'engineered' culture – the company ideology or official version of reality – through presentations, vision statements, work manuals, etc. But culture management isn't just about socializing employees to carry out their work and behave in specific ways, it's also about shaping employee identity in the corporate image. Indeed, many critically oriented studies of culture argue that organization culture is an insidious form of manipulation designed to control the hearts, minds, bodies and souls of employees. Let's take a number of Microsoft's company values as an example: 'A passion for technology, respectful and open, accountable, honest and with integrity, self-critical, and eager to take on big challenges'.[1] We might not quibble with these values *per se*, but they raise an interesting question: Am I being manipulated if, as an employee, I have to be passionate (or at least display passion) about my work? This means thinking, feeling and behaving in ways I might not think or feel, but if I'm going to be evaluated and rewarded based on the degree to which I'm 'passionate', what do I do? Okay, this might seem cynical, but thinking about this reflexively suggests that managing culture could be perceived as controlling the thoughts, desires and experiences of organizational members.

As Kunda argues, the organizational self (employee identity) is not an autonomous self, but is subject to normative controls (organizational norms and values) aimed at eliminating the fragmentation, contradiction and struggle for meaning and identity inherent to organizational life. He found that while most of the employees in the organization seemingly accepted the culture, they were at the same time wary and often cynical about it, and although there were *interpretive struggles* over expectations, deviants were silenced, marginalized or became nonpersons by being moved out of the organization or to less meaningful or influential jobs. Thus, your identity as an employee is a 'managed' one. The idea of the organizational self brings to mind the experience of a student of mine who had a six-month internship in a sales company. The company had regular monthly review meetings at which each person's targets and actual sales for the period were announced. Those who exceeded their target were greeted with wild applause, those who hadn't with boos. Many of the sales staff lived in the same apartment complex and socialized as a group. Despite being offered a permanent job with a great salary, she ended up taking a less well-paid position because she felt uncomfortable with the normative demands and the pressures to conform – not just at work but also spilling over into the personal lives of employees. She was unwilling to participate, saying 'It's just not who I am.'

Even anthropologists are not immune from the charges of the manipulation of culture. In 2000, a controversy exploded over a well-known 1960s study of the Venezuelan Yanomami Indians. Allegations were made about culture manipulation, sexual misconduct, unethical experimentation, the staging of fake villages and the creation of conflict for the purpose of filming the supposedly natural fierce behaviours of the Yanomami people.[2] You might think that manipulating people and staging culture has nothing to do with organizations – but recall how the US energy company Enron managed to hide billions of dollars of debt and operating losses by creating fake partnerships and a fake trading room (complete with ringing phones and family photos on desks) where employees pretended to buy and sell energy contracts during a credit rating visit from Wall Street analysts.[3] This might seem an extreme example, but such front stage performances do occur in many organizations, not necessarily with the intention of being deliberately fraudulent, but with the purpose of managing impressions, which in Goffman's terms can be both deliberate and habitual. I'm reminded of the numerous planning meetings and rehearsals I've attended over the years as part of the preparation for performances deemed necessary for Business School accreditation visits!

This may leave us with rather a dark and cynical view of managers as manipulators of culture and people. It's not meant to be so. What these ideas offer is a different way of thinking about organizational life and what it is that managers may intentionally and unintentionally do; of not taking things for granted, but reflexively questioning various interpretations of organizational life, the part managers play in these interpretations, and possible re-interpretations of more ethical and responsive ways of managing. So in this chapter we'll explore some different ways of thinking about managing organizations through the themes of obversion, subversion and diversion. I use these terms with a sense of irony, because they could be seen as catchy buzzwords (well ... maybe only to a few academics!), but also as a way of taking a critical perspective on a number of management issues – a critically reflexive interrogation of managing culture and an exploration of different ways of thinking about managing organizations.

obversion

> *Rather than seeking definitions and moving to categorize, we should ask: what are we able to see or think about if we talk about it in this way rather than that?*
>
> *Alvesson and Deetz, 2000: 43*

Why obversion? Well, because it draws together two strands we discussed in Chapters 1 and 2. First, Derrida's notions of *différance* and *deconstruction,* the idea that words derive meaning from their opposite term, and as those oppositions always interweave it's important to consider alternative readings. Second, the idea that as reflexive practitioners managers need to question and interrogate taken-for-granted ways of thinking and acting. The obverse is an opposite or a counterpart to something – but is both opposite and complementary. So we'll look at three major issues of relevance to managing organizations today – managing culture, power and authority, and the gendered and embodied nature of management. We'll look at them differently from the way they are normally treated, yet this way of thinking about these issues is integral to managing because they reflect the way that some people experience culture, power and gender.

managing culture

In Chapter 2, we unsettled a few basic assumptions about language, communication and management, and looked at some different ideas based on the view that language *is* our world and that our everyday ways of talking are crucial. Within organization studies, managing culture is one of the few fields where academics and managers alike recognize the importance of language. Managers and organizational consultants spend a lot of time and energy coming up with compelling (that is, appropriately worded to generate commitment) vision, mission and value statements to create a culture of empowerment, innovation, excellent customer service, ——— … fill in the gap. Academics taking a whole range of epistemological perspectives study the relationship between language and organization culture: realists examine how a real existing culture is expressed (represented) through stories, slogans, speeches, jargon and symbols, etc.; social constructionists explore how language shapes 'culture' and identities; poststructuralists deconstruct culture to expose its empty, fragmented and contested nature – the struggles over meaning. Let's look at some different ways of viewing the management of organizational culture: managing discourse, managing the hyperreal, and managing communities of difference.

managing culture as discourse
The study of organizational discourse emerged from the social constructionist emphasis on language: that organizations are created

through discourse. Discourse is viewed as naturally occurring talk (conversations – primary speech genres), written text (e.g., emails, documents, statements on company websites), semiotics (physical artifacts and visual images), ways of looking at and talking about the world (Discourse with a capital 'D' – secondary speech genres), and also social action. Linguist Norman Fairclough, who has written extensively in this area, suggests that discourse is 'simultaneously a piece of text, an instance of discursive practice, and an instance of social practice' (1992: 4). While we tend to think of text as something pretty much fixed, Fairclough (2003) suggests we create meaning through *texturing*, a process of drawing on different texts and semiotic elements in our conversations; about combining global and broader social Discourses with local discourses to create and enact new discourses. It's a process in which meaning gets concurrently multiplied and sharpened as we identify new alternatives and come to share agreement. From this perspective, it doesn't make sense to talk about organizations as static entities or structures, but as continual processes of organizing in which organizational members create some sort of shared meaning about what needs to be done. We not only shape meaning and coordinate action on a day-to-day basis, but identities, strategy, learning, change, etc., emerge within organizational discourses.

Organizational D/discourse also encompasses *semiotics*, the study of the relationship between meanings and signs, both linguistic and non-linguistic, texts and symbols. A symbol is a signifier because it works as a visual representation conveying meaning – an object, a sound, a form of dress, gesture and emotion. Think of the five interlocking rings of the Olympics representing the union of five continents, or the Mercedes logo and the regal purple colour used by Cadbury, both of which signify quality. Interestingly, Baudrillard suggests that we consume signs and images that are important not because of their use, but for the image they offer. I don't buy a Mercedes just for the purpose of transporting me from A to B, but because it creates an image that I'm rich, urbane and distinctive … (not that I have a Mercedes!).

Managers manage symbols as part of the process of managing culture and meaning, and symbolic meaning can draw on the emotions, as the example below from a conversation with a US Federal Security Director of a US airport illustrates:

FSD: See this lanyard? It says 'Team ———'.
ANN: Uhuh.
FSD: If you go out, the screeners all have 'Team ———' on the back of their shirts. I want to say, 'Hey – we're in this together', and what happened in New York on September 11th – we can never ever let that happen again. And we can *only* do it if we work together. You know, the adage about a chain being only as strong as it's weakest link...

Of course, as we saw in Chapter 2, meaning is context-dependent and variable, so the semiotic meaning attributed to these artifacts may vary across employees, passengers, and other airport staff. But the importance to the Director of getting some sort of shared meaning really struck me when he commented that he felt personally responsible for the passengers in each plane that took off from his airport.

If we think about organizational culture as an interweaving of Discourses and discourse, what does this mean? That managers need to pay attention to language and how meanings and actions are created and maintained through written texts, symbols and everyday conversations. It means not thinking about organizations as fixed, bounded and unitary structures, culture and systems, but as processes of organizing, emerging and open to many interpretations and reinterpretations in lived experience. We've already emphasized a number of distinctions and their impact: organization and or organizing, management/managing, texts/texturing, monologue/dialogue. As Karl Weick (1995) says, organizations as structures only exist in retrospective sensemaking, organizing is what we do every day in our actions and our talk. It's the 'ing' part that makes a difference because it means that it's important for managers to recognize that managing, organizing and sensemaking occur *all the time* in our actions and conversations – whether or not we are aware of 'doing' them. Language is important.

managing the hyperreal

We talked about performativity in Chapter 1, the idea that we talk and act things into being. French social philosopher Jean Baudrillard takes performativity further, arguing that it is no longer possible to talk about what is real. In his 1994 book *Simulacra and Simulations*, he claimed that the distinction between the real and the sign or image has broken down, and that there isn't a real original any more – just an image that masks the absence of reality. Simulacra can be nostalgic – trying to reproduce a lost reality, such as the reproduction of an organization culture of traditional family values when the original family who started and built the organization is no longer involved. Simulacra can also be a simulation of an ideal or the not-yet-real, a company, the media, or a government presenting information and images to create an event or situation that doesn't exist. Baudrillard calls this *hyperreality*, an interactive performance or simulation in which we are trying to produce what we think is real, but which is only an image.

Imagine working in a large glass-clad structure built to eliminate boundaries and bring you closer to the customer and community by blending the inside and outside. An open plan design with no interior walls, and with modern chrome and glass furniture. You are expected to dress, talk and act in particular ways, to have the 'WOW!' factor: to be creative, fun, happy, helpful and do what it takes to put internal and external customers first. This is hyperreality, and is different from Goffman's performance in at least one essential way: for Baudrillard the simulation becomes the real, the distinction breaks down between the sign and the signified, the fake and the authentic. You walk through the door and instinctively become the WOW! person: the successful manipulation of culture, of identity, and of hearts, minds and souls.

managing relationally: culture as communities of difference

Linguistic anthropologist Michael Agar has an interesting view of culture. He says that we tend to think of culture as some *thing* that groups of people have. Culture tells us who we are; it's about our national, organizational or group identity, and it's also about how the world works – how we interact with each other, what we value, and how we see the rest of the world. But culture is more than that; it's also about how we relate to others, 'what happens to *you* when you encounter differences, become aware of something in yourself, and work to figure out why the differences appeared. Culture is an awareness, a consciousness, one that reveals the hidden self and opens paths to other ways of being' (1994: 20) – and it happens in language. In other words, as we encounter different cultures, national or otherwise, we realize that people have different ways of seeing the world, different speech genres, meanings and ways of talking – not just different languages. This brings us back to Bakhtin's notion of heteroglossia, the importance of recognizing the many languages, speech genres, meanings, ways of talking and of seeing – and of employing speech tact. As he says:

> The better our command of genres, the more freely we employ them, the more fully we reveal our own individuality in them (where this is possible and necessary), the more flexibly and precisely we reflect the unrepeatable situation of communication – in a word, the more perfectly we implement our free speech plan. (1986: 80)

Agar's ideas become relevant to managers when he talks about how we deal with the differences within a multicultural world. Some people see difference as a threat and take a deficit approach to dealing with the situation – what does the other culture or person lack when compared to me and my (superior) culture, and how do I remedy that? This involves a monologic process of socialization and colonization: expecting or requiring the 'other' to subordinate their values, beliefs and actions to mine. If you've experienced a company merger or acquisition, you may be familiar with this deficit process as one culture subsumes the other. Colonization can also occur on a one-to-one basis between managers and employees from different ethnicities, races and genders.

Others recognize that differences are rich opportunities to learn something about ourselves and others, because differences make us aware not only of what we take for granted in our own culture, but also of new ways of seeing, saying and doing. In comparing the two approaches, Agar asks, 'In a business negotiation where X knows a great deal about Y, and Y knows almost nothing about X, who has the advantage?' (p. 24). It's an instrumental question, but a crucial one that managers can ask at many levels: substitute 'a business negotiation' with: a merger of two companies, a market, a team, or an interaction with a staff member...

So managing culture can be a means of control and manipulation, of managing identities, hearts and minds, and of making all employees the same, as Kunda suggests. But Agar's view of culture as difference offers a way of moving past control and colonization to *acculturation*. By figuring out how we connect and how we differ, we can employ that 'free speech plan' and build on the connections and differences to remain distinct and yet changed in some way. Understanding culture as difference offers opportunities for managing people and organizations in more responsive and ethical ways, and reframes managing as a relational practice, and managers as cultural explorers and adventurers, rather than manipulators.

'i got the power'… and the authority and the responsibility

> And when they go to their bosses, they say, 'I don't want to know about layouts! I don't want to resolve the issues with the lawyers', who all work for Corporate. Literally, none of the lawyers can make a decision for the rest of the group, and there are 8 lawyers. We have to talk to every single one to get agreement. And there's no leverage! And I think there are a lot of groups around here where it's a similar kind of thing. Information Technology has a steering committee that is trying to look out into the future. To what degree do people say, 'Yes, I agree to give my authority to the steering committee and abide by its decisions'? (Programme Manager talking about authority issues in a project)

Organizations run on authority structures, and one of the first things you learn on Management 101, is the relationship between authority, responsibility and accountability. Scholars in the era of the systematization of management were concerned with clarifying and establishing managerial authority and differentiating managers from others through the nature of their responsibility. Authority is typically seen as the right to give orders and to enforce rules – it's about legitimate power – monologic ways of speaking. Responsibility is the obligation to achieve goals, make specified decisions, and perform certain tasks, for which you are held accountable, that is, answerable to your boss. The key is ensuring that a manager's authority is commensurate with responsibility, so that she or he has the power to get things done.

However, as you can see in the above quote from the Programme Manager, power is complex: it not only involves authority and responsibility, it also requires establishing relationships, getting commitment, and persuading others over whom you have no authority. And, as you might now imagine, there are different views on what power is, how it plays out in practice, and who should have it. From a rational and realist perspective, power is vested in a hierarchical position, is a manager's prerogative, and managerial authority is unquestionably legitimate. Critical scholars challenge the distribution of power throughout society, and the right of particular groups (owners, shareholders, managers) to dominate and control others. From a social constructionist perspective, power is embedded within social practices and relationships. Other than giving a brief overview, I don't want to spend too much time talking about rational and realist constructions of power, authority and responsibility, because you can read about these in any management book. I do want to explore some alternative ways of thinking about these issues that offer possibilities for managing differently.

the power and the glory...

In mainstream management and organization theory, managers (as rational agents) are apportioned the right to have authority over others, with a corresponding responsibility for outcomes. Power is some-*thing* associated with a particular position and level in an organization, and authority often draws on Max Weber's idea of rational-legal authority. This takes us back to the idea that management is about representing and intervening – specifying rules, procedures, jobs, tasks, goals, and intervening through the division of labour, deskilling work and setting up measurement systems to control employee performance. Power and authority are also represented discursively and semiotically in *talk*, *signs*, *texts* and *symbols*: a manager giving instructions to an employee, a job title, a job description, a large office, a company car and a parking space. Much of the literature in the field is concerned with how managers can influence others and gain power by creating situations where other organizational members are dependent upon them because they have the knowledge, expertise, resources, and/or information that others need, or because they can resolve critical organizational problems (e.g. Kotter, 1977; Pfeffer, 1992; Salancik and Pfeffer, 1977).

From a conventional managerialist perspective, authority is transcendent, legitimate and monologic. By this, I mean that authority is vested in a position regardless of the person holding it; it legitimates the manager's right to control the actions and behaviours of others; and monologic because it establishes who has the right to speak and who doesn't. Bakhtin (1986: 163) suggests the process of monologization occurs when dialogic voices are assimilated into one voice, in this case the managerial voice of authority.

From a critical perspective, rational approaches to authority are processes of distinction and consent, and an effect of historical, economic, political, social and therefore ideological forces. When someone becomes a manager, she or he becomes a member of, and identifies with, a group, a profession or a class that is distinct from other groups – a distinction shaped by history, discourse and social practices, and maintained by those in authority and those under authority. Bakhtin talks about how *authoritative discourse* (for example scientific truth or managerialism) gets its power:

> The authoritative word demands that we acknowledge it, that we make it our own; it binds us, quite independent of any power it might have to persuade us internally; we encounter it with its authority already fused to it. The authoritative word is located in a distanced zone, organically connected with a past that is felt to be hierarchically higher. It is, so to speak, the word of the fathers ... It is therefore not a question of choosing it from among other possible discourses that are its equal. (1981: 342)

In other words, we accept the authority of management discourse and the discourse of management authority, and let these discourses define our ideological relationship with the world: not necessarily because we are persuaded by their legitimacy, but because we take their form of reasoning as a given truth. Such discourses, Bakhtin says, enter our consciousness as static, complete and inflexible – demanding our unconditional allegiance. It was not until the advent of CMS that alternative discourses and new voices emerged engaged in questioning the nature of 'modern' management and organizations.

Which brings us to the idea that critical scholars take a transgressive view of power, arguing that we need to look at alternative readings, at the relationship between control and resistance, domination and submission, and to uncover the insidious nature of power. But why should we consider critiques of power? Because a critically reflexive examination of authority structures and their intended and unintended consequences, can form a basis for discovering more humane ways of managing.

Critical scholars analyse the structural mechanisms, the ideologies and the communication processes that lead to the exploitation of employees, with the aim of creating more democratic forms of governance and working. As we saw in Chapter 1, critics of ideology question the assumption that capitalist and managerialist ideologies legitimate owners' and managers' rights to dominate workers. They also explore how this domination occurs in ways of which we may be unaware. Karl Marx argued that workers participate in their own exploitation by accepting an owner's or a manager's right to give orders. Italian Marxist theorist Antonio Gramsci (1971), used the concept of *hegemony* to explain why this happens, why dominated groups are not necessarily coerced into conforming, but spontaneously and actively consent to being dominated. He claims this is because institutional and ideological values, and the structures, systems and practices that support them, become part of our everyday taken-for-granted activities, and so influence us throughout our life in subtle and incessant ways – they become 'normal' to us.

However ... in succumbing to hegemonic practices they work against our interests by restricting our personal choices. For example, I might be given greater autonomy, a good thing you might think because it means I have discretion over my work. I can do what I want, when I want, and I can manage myself. So I decide to work on some challenging projects that I might otherwise not have done if asked by my manager. I stay late and work over the weekend to finish them. Of course, this benefits my manager and the organization, but I end up with less personal time and spending less and less time with my family. Steven Lukes (1974) calls this insidious form of power the *third face of power* – it doesn't take into consideration divergent values, interests or practices, or alternative ways of organizing work.

Hegemony involves a constant struggle, not just over power, but also over identity. Consider these comments made by an MBA student:

> I had something to prove. Being only 27 ... no military background, did not graduate from an Ivy League or equivalent, and worked for a

family business ... In addition, I carried the baggage of racial and economic discrimination from both my parents' and personal experiences. I realize now that I suffered from a poor self-image. I had an inferiority complex that fueled my passion and work ethic. I needed to prove that I was better than my white, Ivy League, affluent, experienced peers. If they were smarter, then I would work harder. But I would be damned to concede that they were any better.

These comments illustrate that hegemony is not an abstract concept, but rather it's a lived experience that involves the control of emotions, hearts and minds; how hegemony is an attempt to ignore distinctions in order to maintain power; and how in this case resistance is ironically a form of compliance that benefits the very group the student was resisting and to which he felt he had something to prove – something he discovered later when he found his manager taking the recognition for his work. His comments also illustrate the frustration that can occur when managers remain insensitive to difference.

the relational nature of responsibility

I've been advocating that managers should manage in ethical and responsible ways, and so far avoided talking about what that means, apart from suggesting that reflexivity is a key element. We'll look at ethics in the next chapter, but now let us look at some of the different ways of constructing 'responsibility'. In particular, I want to offer a relational and dialogic view of responsibility that takes into account the need to be open to others, to various voices and meanings, and to the need for dialogue and discussion as an integral part of responsive and ethical management.

Responsibility is one of those key words in management: managers are responsible for achieving goals by the most effective and efficient means possible, for managing budgets, etc. This corresponds to the idea of the manager as rational agent, responsible for work outcomes and for the job performance of subordinates. Rational constructions of responsibility are couched in such a way that they often lead to feelings of liability – that as a manager I have a legal responsibility to make sure the work gets done, my employees work in a safe environment and so on, because if I don't there will be consequences I'll have to face. This doesn't necessarily give me a personal sense of responsibility as a manager, but rather a duty of responsibility – something I'm obliged to do. But I have been using the term responsibility in a different sense: one that focuses on the *response* part of the word, and one that offers a very different way of thinking about who we are and what we say and do as managers.

In Chapter 2 we talked about relationally *respons*ive dialogue and how our everyday conversations entail an intuitive as well as a more deliberate *respons*iveness to the words, gestures and feelings of others. Which means that we have a responsibility to consider and *respond* to others – *to be responsive, responsible and accountable to others in our everyday interactions with them*. This reconstruction emphasizes the embedded and relational nature of responsibility. Responsibility is not just something that is formalized or legalized in specific items identified on a job description or in policy and procedure documents, but situated in our everyday relationships – in which we are responsible to and with others. Contrast also the language 'responsible for…' and 'responsible to and with …'. The latter implies we can't avoid responsibility because it's implicit in our interactions with other people. Avoiding responsibility means denying the very sociality of our existence, because everything we say and do is in relation to others. So, as we interact, we have a responsibility to each other, to listen, to consider and to respond in appropriate and respectful ways. This way of thinking about responsibility is crucial to managing as practical authors and reflexive practitioners because it means thinking about how our assumptions influence what we say or might not say, and how others might respond. As we will see in the next chapter, it draws on existential and phenomenological conceptions. When Sartre says we are 'condemned to be free' (1956: 529) he is arguing it is so because we are responsible for making choices about who we are, what to do, and for others – and in those choices lie both uncertainties and opportunities to realize our being. Life is not easy.

gender, man-agement and man-agers

> *Yet our direct experience tells us that organizational cultures – as holistic phenomena – are strongly 'gendered'. Organizations themselves, therefore, are gendered, and organizational processes are ways of organizing gender relations.*
>
> *Gherardi, 1995: 12*

I've mentioned before the gendered nature of management and organizations, I've hinted and dissembled, so let's get to the nub – what does this mean? The first thought on gender is often that it's about the position and pay of women in organizations. Recent surveys show that gender inequality still exists. The UK's 2008 *Sex and Power Report* found that women make up only 11 per cent of FTSE directors, 19.3 per cent of MPs, and at director level the gender pay gap is around 22 per cent. Comparing the average pay for men and women we find that in the UK women earn around 88 pence to the male pound, in the USA women earn 77 cents to every male dollar, and in Australia only 34 per cent of women are managers, and on average women earn 84 cents compared to the male dollar.[4] The number of sexual discrimination lawsuits filed in the US has been pretty constant for the last 10 years. For example, in 2007 the US Equal Employment Opportunities Commission filed a lawsuit against Bloomberg for demoting and reducing the salaries of three high-level female executives who were pregnant. But the statistics are only part of the story, because numbers objectify the embodied lived experience of gendered work and organizations.

Gendered organizations are not just about numbers and whether the organization has day-care facilities, but also about who is in power, who does what type of work, what normative expectations influence behaviour and attitudes, what type of language is spoken, and how organizational members are evaluated, rewarded and promoted. Organizations are gendered linguistically, semiotically and practically, in taken-for-granted ways of acting and being. Practically, particular types of work are typically seen as women's work (the caring professions: secretarial, nursing, teaching), and women play supportive roles as secretaries and assistants to a patriarchal social order of male dominance. Women as well as men often take for granted what is accepted as 'the norm' and what is enacted as being different. As critical communication theorists Karen Ashcraft and Dennis Mumby say: 'Put simply, women appear as visibly gendered "others", while men are erased as the genderless norm' (2004: xiv). In other words, the 'white maleness' of organizations remains unquestioned, while non-white, non-maleness is emphasized through activities such as the setting up of women and minority advisory committees and mentor networks. In effect, such committees and networks reinforce power inequalities and boundaries because they are outside the 'normal' structure and practice, and serve to differentiate and exclude groups rather than include them.

This process of differentiation was really brought home in the way the media (both men and women) treated Hillary Clinton during her run for the Presidential candidacy. Watch the video montage of the media treatment of Hillary Clinton,[5] which includes comments such as: 'Her hair looked great', 'If she knew how it made her look ...', 'Men won't vote for Hillary Clinton because she reminds them of their nagging wives', 'The reason she's a US senator, the reason she's a candidate for President ... is her husband messed around ... She didn't win on her merit', and so on. Were the same comments being made about her male counterparts?! This seemingly egregious – yet frighteningly real – example highlights women as 'visibly gendered others'.

We encountered the gendered, ethnocentric and performative nature of Management Discourse in Chapter 1 – how the ever-present discourse of rationality requires masculine skills and forms of behaviour (control, authority, discipline, objectivity, individuality, competitiveness, assertiveness, and so on) that non-male, non-white employees are often expected to emulate. The role of Discourse (language systems) and discourse (everyday ways of talking) in reinforcing gendered norms can be seen in the way pregnancy was treated in the US. From the 1960s onwards, pregnancy was classed legally as a *temporary disability* in which pregnant women could not be treated any more or less favourably than employees with other disabilities. Business associations argued that health insurance and disability plans should not be extended to cover pregnancy and childbirth, because childbirth was a voluntary condition! In addition, the definition of a disability as a physical or mental impairment that substantially limits carrying out normal life activities, frames childbirth as a non-normal event that lessens a woman's ability to carry out her work in quality ways and continue to be committed to the organization. It wasn't until the 1993 Family and Medical Leave Act that both male and female employees had the right to take unpaid leave to care for the birth, adoption or foster care of her or his child.

Table 3   Discursive positions of women in a male culture

Friendly cultures	*Women as guests*: treated politely, being protected and looked after, yet given women's tasks (talking to people on the phone) and always in a subordinated position.
	Women as holidaymakers: seen as just passing through, conforming to past practices, not feeling 'at home' and thus not able to change things.
	Women as newcomers: seen as a curiosity, but not as 'a real man'. Judged on her ability to integrate.
Hostile cultures	*Women as marginal*: tolerated yet invisible, expected to obey, agree and wait for decisions, not allowed to question or contribute to discussions.
	Women as the snake in the grass: seen as the enemy who confronts and changes the 'normal' rather than conforming.
	Women as intruders: who position themselves as equal yet who are actively resisted by others.

Source: Based on Gherardi (1995: 108–22)

Organization sociologist Silvia Gherardi (1995) suggests that the presence of women, especially in male-gendered cultures, involves both men and women in the 'remedial work' of restoring gendered order. She uses a storied or narrative approach to talk about how women deal with D/discourses of femaleness within organizational D/discourses of maleness that can be friendly or hostile (see Table 3).

These are discursive and relational positions in that they are enacted, resisted, negotiated, and perhaps changed in the everyday interactions of both male and female organizational members. The discursive construction of gender in male-gendered cultures was also evident in the 'Blair's Babes' label given to the 101 women MPs elected in the 1997 UK election. This slang term, meaning a naïve attractive woman, is a debasing construction that has practical implications for the way women are treated – where were 'Blair's Dudes'?

The lived experience of gender at work is also about linguistic oppositions: we talk about 'hard' technical skills versus 'soft' people skills, public versus private, rational versus emotional, and so on – oppositions associated with being masculine or feminine, in which one is privileged over the other. This oppositional way of seeing situations, and the

tensions this can raise for women managers can be seen in the comment
by a female manager during our discussion about her work:

> I was talking to someone today who said they'd heard that I was one
> of those women who's tough for the sake of being tough, but that
> actually they thought I was very nice! And I said, 'Oh? Okay!' I had
> two reactions to it; one is that it means you are the virgin or the
> whore – as a woman you either get to be tough or nice but somehow
> you can't be both ...

Others share her experience of the tensions of gendered identity. In
her study of women managers in the public sector, Joanna Brewis
(1999) found that women downplayed signifiers of their sex by dress-
ing in more masculine ways (tailored suits and jackets), by not being
too attractive yet being seen to be in control of their bodies (not too
fat, too small), by being 'one of the boys' while not being too masculine, and by knowing when to flirt and when not. Brewis examines
how women deal with the tensions of masculinity and femininity so
that they can actively participate in predominantly masculine cultures. She also points out the complexities of managing their bodies
and emotions, a point reinforced by Nancy Harding (2002), who
talks about the social semiotics of managers' bodies, both male and
female, as a form of shorthand managerial discourse. The subjectified
or performative body of the manager is a black suit, tie, clean-shaven,
'ascetic, neat, disciplined, controlled, leak-proof – but always masculine and always potent' (p. 68). An ironically emotionless and neutral
body designed to control nature and symbolize being organized and
the organization. Thus, the body is not only visibly gendered, but also
a site of subordination to organizational ideals, and when female
managers draw upon masculine signifiers as a way of participating,
this reinforces the gendered discourse of management, identity and
organizations (Pullen, 2006).

Gender also plays out practically in different conversational styles.
Linguist Deborah Tannen (1995, 2001) has done a considerable
amount of work in this area, finding that men and women talk differently. Men say 'I', speak directly, position themselves as in authority,
and talk about their achievements. Women say 'we', question, speak
tentatively, are concerned with relationships, and dislike boasting.

These different ways of talking have very practical implications in terms of whose comments are more likely to be recognized, remembered and rewarded.

Gender is a key concern of critical management studies, and there are many other aspects to be considered if we had the space to do so.[6] We've just touched the surface in this chapter. Nevertheless, the gendered and racialized nature of organizations is a key aspect of critical management that needs ongoing reflexive interrogation. The gendered structuring of organizations is performative: gender differences are created and maintained in organizational Discourse and everyday interactions, a process of social construction in which both men and women produce and reproduce gender distinctions in conscious or unconscious ways by uncritically enacting and accepting those differences. In this sense, gender is embedded in historical, social and organizational D/discourse, an ever-present hegemonic aspect of culture that can exclude people. It is an integral part of the monologic practice of *man*agement and *man*aging that we need to open to reflexive critique.

subversion

L.:   My predecessor had a picture on the wall – it was a team thing – one of those hunting metaphors with male hunters chasing men in deer-skins (our competitors) – but it was so male and they didn't get it.

ANN: The images of aggression and masculinity?

L.:   Yes, and in meetings they use baseball and football metaphors – so I thought I'm not using any sporting metaphors, I'm creating my own.

Subversion implies the undermining or overthrowing of something – at a minimum it implies non-compliance and, beyond this, rebellion or revolution. Critical Management Studies is not just about obversion – understanding the taken-for-granted power structures and hegemonic practices that lead to intended and unintended injustices of modern management – but also about finding ways of destabilizing, subverting and changing those injustices. Of course, not every manager in every organization is deliberately engaging in oppressive actions, but managing critically means being reflexive about our assumptions, relationships, interactions, and about management practice at large. It's about knowing what is and what is not ethical. The quote above, an excerpt from a research conversation with a female manager, highlights the power relationships and gender differences embedded within everyday symbols and conversations that are a taken-for-granted part of organizational life. Her response was a linguistic act of resistance. Forms of resistance are a central concern within critical approaches. In this section, we'll look at ways in which both managers and employees resist what they feel are threats to their identity and sense of self. We will take a social constructionist perspective, which sees resistance as constructed within the talk and the interactions of organizational participants – participants who themselves will have differing interpretations of what is 'real'.

⬤ discursive resistance

The comments made by L. (above) about sports metaphors and cartoons illustrate the discursive and symbolic aspects of hegemony. Ernest Laclau and Chantal Mouffe (1985) suggest that discursive hegemony occurs when one discourse prevails and becomes the dominant interpretive framework through which conversations, actions and identities pass and become redefined. Hegemony is spatial and symbolic in the sense that space and place structure our interactions (such as assembly lines, cubicles), are saturated with semiotic meanings (for example, a large corner office, type and size of desk and chair) and therefore maintain distinctions of power and identity. Such meanings will vary according to the background conversations of organizational members, conversations that 'constitute different realities for their participants. And there is a particular coherence given by the background conversations such that within that reality, everything is appropriate' (Ford, Ford and McNamara, 2002). Andrew Brown and Michael Humphreys (2006) studied discursive resistance to spatial hegemony in a UK college. They found that different groups discursively constructed the college as a place of work in very different ways in their background conversations: a place with purpose, as a problem/prison, as rational/irrational, as symbolic of failure/takeover, as a place of nostalgia and of fantasy and future. These competing discursive constructions of space were closely linked with promoting and protecting preferred group identities and with resisting hegemony. Managers need to be sensitive to the interpretive struggles within background conversation, to the ways in which different groups and individuals talk about situations and experiences, how these ways of talking might be tied to identity, and how different meanings may be recognized and accepted.

⬤ identity, emotion and resistance

And this brings us to a point that I've been careful to emphasize throughout the book. That whether we are managers or employees, we cannot separate ourselves and our relationships with others from our work. What we do, how we act, and how we think about our work, how we interact with others, is closely tied with our identity – with who we are. Many of the managers' and students' comments I've included are statements of identity: of emotional struggles with identity at an individual or a collective level. The relationship between emotion and identity at work is a crucial one for managers to understand, but one that's often ignored. For the rational manager, emotions are to be erased, masked or managed in organizational life. We rarely consider emotion on management courses, and if we do it's often in a disembodied way as 'emotional intelligence' (something a manager needs to have) or 'emotional labour', which is about being required to display specific emotions on the job. Arlie Hochschild's 1983 study of Delta Airline flight attendants drew attention to emotional labour, the idea that emotions are turned into commodities from which the organization can profit. She found that flight attendants were required to 'love the job' and to smile. They were trained to manage and project required emotions, and in anger-desensitization. Some employees coped with the emotional requirements by separating their 'real' and 'fake' selves, but then had to deal with feelings that they were being insincere. Managing hearts, minds and bodies has emotional consequences for those being managed.

This experience is shared across a range of service jobs and in the caring professions where emotions – being happy, interested in customers, concerned about client problems, friendly, sympathetic, etc., are part of the front stage performance. It's interesting to note that women are often perceived at being better at work that requires emotional labour, and that many of these professions are feminized. Mirchandani (2003) found that women small business owners did a considerable amount of emotion work – managing their own and others' (customers', business partners') emotions. But, significantly, she discovered that immigrant women and women of colour managed their emotions in very different ways to white women, and also found themselves managing identity 'relations of difference', in that customers saw them as non-white women capable only of manual, repetitive and low status work. Her findings have implications for the ways in which we manage because they suggest that we need to be sensitive not only to differences, but also to the way we respond to those differences.

In her study of female engineers, Joyce Fletcher (1998) found that the women themselves managed their own difference. Many engaged in *relational practices*, which in this sense are seen as feminine beliefs centring around the idea that development occurs through mutual empathy and empowerment rather than individual competitiveness. In the work setting, relational practices included preserving the well-being of a project, enabling oneself and others to contribute to projects, and working collaboratively in teams. Each of these required being sensitive to the emotional aspects of interactions. However, the dominant organizational D/discourse recognized and rewarded autonomy, self-promotion and individual heroics – and relational practice was ignored, seen as 'mothering', or exploited by the male engineers. Rather than resist the prevailing D/discourse, the female engineers, while wanting to work differently, *disappeared* relational practices, which included talking about relational behaviours as weak and inappropriate for work, and warning female colleagues of the consequences of engaging in these behaviours. The implications of Fletcher's work are clear: managerial practices continue to reinforce gendered definitions of competence and success that exclude other equally valid ways of contributing. Even though many organizations are moving towards empowerment and team-based approaches, unless managers recognize the ways of relating, talking and interacting necessary to support the change, they will likely fail.

In contrast, a study by Hester Eisenstein (1996) of women in government positions in Australia, found a group of senior women (named femocrats) engaged in enacting policies that advanced women's interests in a bureaucracy and a policy environment that reflected men's interests. It's a fascinating study of how a group of women with an agenda of social change, managed to deal with the contradictions and tensions of remaining both active feminists and 'good bureaucrats'. Although criticized by the political Right for being too radical, and by the women's movement for not being radical enough, this group of influential women challenged the male power structure in state bureaucracy. They set up a central women's affairs office for policy purposes, had a clear agenda for change, and won funding for women's initiatives. A strategy of resistance through coordinated action.

humour

Humour often provides a form of resistance, and can be seen as the part of organizational life that Yiannis Gabriel (1995) suggests is, and should be, unmanageable. The unmanaged organization reflects a spontaneous, emotional, *fantasy* life of stories, gossip and jokes: fantasy in that stories of real events are embellished and imbued with different meanings and significance. I'm reminded of an event that occurred years ago at my place of work. A senior manager got her hand stuck in the coffee vending machine, reaching up to pull down a miscreant cup. The Fire Brigade arrived to cut her hand out, followed by an ambulance and a police car. The manager was rather an autocratic and exacting person, the bane of trainee lives because they felt she monitored their every move. The irony of the situation was not lost upon them, and the story took on epic proportions, including the manager ostensibly being carried out of the building by a burly fireman. Trainees were careful to ensure they had a cup of vending machine coffee when attending meetings with her. This unmanaged space not only incorporated stories and humour as a form of resistance, which Gabriel suggests is often a response to being over-managed and over-controlled, but helped trainees cope with what were often demanding and stressful interactions, and gave them a sense of connection with each other. But humour as resistance isn't confined to employees. Damian Hodgson (2005) found that both managers and employees expected to conform to newly implemented professional project management procedures and methods dealt with their anxiety by parodying and mocking such methods, and in the process distanced themselves from the methods and found a degree of shared security.

Acts of resistance can also be practical. They don't have to take the form of open rebellion but can be more subtle, such as withdrawing effort or engaging in theft, dishonesty or sabotage. Prasad and Prasad (2001) found routine acts of resistance to the computerization of work in a health care organization. While the official management position was that there was no formal resistance, managers recognized that employees engaged in mundane acts of resistance such as 'careful carelessness' (spilling coffee on keyboards, forgetting to save data, accidentally misfiling information), sabotage, and 'dumb resistance' (such as a reluctance to use personal judgement). The artful subversion of managerial authority took on heroic proportions among employees, and managers found it difficult to deal with actions that could be perceived as being unintentional.

The point that I hope to make here is that if we consider managing as an oppositional practice, an ongoing tension between managers and employees, organization and disorganization, managed and unmanaged, power and resistance, feminine and masculine, and so on, then issues of culture, power, identity, gender and language become interrelated and multifaceted aspects of managing organizations. Therefore, managers need to be aware of the invisible and moral, as well as the visible and seemingly benign, aspects: to be sensitive to the tensions and relationship with the 'other', to what is said and unsaid, and to be open to the possibilities for change that difference offers.

diversion

Issues of diversity are very personal and unless you confront them in a personal way, organizations just aren't going to get anywhere. It's about how do I get L—— to fit into this white, male-oriented organization – because there *is* going to come a point at which I say: No! I'm not going to give up who I am to do that. The question to me is to what degree does the organization want me or other kinds of people, and be willing to accept there are other ways of behaving and acting and to become more cognizant that there are norms that are culturally based and gender based, and the advantage of having women in the organization and respecting differences ... Unless the organization is open to that, it is not going to be especially effective. (Female Project Manager in a large high-tech company)

What are those possibilities for change? I'd like to end this chapter by looking at some different considerations in managing organizations.

⬤ managing difference or making a difference?

Managing difference is not about minimizing difference – the deficit model, that is, how can you adapt and be integrated into my way of doing things, because you are going to be evaluated on these criteria? Neither is it training people to think and act like the norm through such programmes as 'Dress for success' or 'Communicating assertively'. Most management techniques, processes and procedures are concerned with reducing people to the same, events to their simplest common denominator, or projects to their critical elements. Maslow's Hierarchy of Needs (1943) is a classic example of a general theory of motivation that makes assumptions about how everyone should behave and what their purpose in life should be – to self-actualize. What we've seen is that reducing life to generalizations misses a great deal. Organizations are not simple structures but complex interweavings of people and their emotions, meanings, interpretations, actions, assumptions, bodies and ways of talking that often favour one group over another ... Managing is complex, and reducing it to techniques is not practical because managing is not an 'it' – managing is about who managers are and how they relate with other people in relationally responsive dialogue. Managing is both a reflexive and a dialectical practice in the sense that managers, along with other members of the organization, shape and maintain 'organizational practices' in their everyday interactions and conversations. Managers therefore need to be self reflexive about the impact of their assumptions and ways of speaking and relating, and critically reflexive about managerial ideologies, organizational discourse and practices.

Managers who are reflexive practitioners also look for differences between their espoused theories and theories-in-action, between what they say and what they do.[7] For example, Jackie Ford's (2006) study of male and female public sector managers, found masculine macho discourses of leadership (competitive, performance measurement driven) were still valued in practice, despite a more espoused feminine rhetoric or postheroic discourse (listening, collaborative). The managers dealt with this ambiguity and complexity by adopting a range of subject positions such as a caring collaborative approach and an arrogant autocratic approach. One of my students commented on a similar experience – that despite an organizational rhetoric of transformational leadership, and managers going through intensive training to become transformational leaders, a survey of employees showed no indication that the approach had been implemented.

Let's take Mike Agar's notion of culture as difference and Bakhtin's notion of language and dialogism, and see what they might have to offer us in terms of managing organizations. If we accept the ideas presented in Chapter 2 that we dialectically shape our social realities and that language is crucial to this process, then we can reframe organizations as constantly emerging relational language communities that we create and maintain in our everyday interactions and conversations. But they are also, as we have seen, communities of difference, of heteroglossia: where our sense of organizational life, of ourselves, and of what needs to be done, is contested, negotiated and created between us in our relationally responsive dialogical activities. 'Features' of the organization (strategy, goals, plans, etc.) are not 'objects', but partially shared ways of talking and acting that serve to both unify and pull apart meanings. Organizational features, texts, symbols and signs can be interpreted differently by different people, and so it's important for managers to look at how language is used in the organization, and what it tells us about how people experience organizational life in similar and different ways. Managers who are attuned to heteroglossia are sensitive to different and competing voices, to what is said as well as the silences, and to the impact of monologic ways of talking and acting. They focus on relating across difference and the many individual voices in our community and conversations – in Bakhtin's terms, *polyphony*.

But what might this look like in an organization? The notion of polyphony is one often taken up by feminist scholars concerned with different ways of managing and organizing; where dialogue and polyphony are seen as participation, minimizing rules and maximizing personal choice, and offering options rather than instructions. Karen Ashcraft (2001a, 2001b) places feminist ways of organizing as feminist discourse communities. In her study of an organization run by women for battered women she found that even though a formal hierarchical structure existed on paper, power relationships were minimized in favour of empowerment. Rules were kept to essential concerns (such as client confidentiality), power relations still existed but attempts to balance these were made by using 'we' (rather than 'I') and aiming for consensus. This was supported by a D/discourse of *ethical communication* in which the goal was both client and employee empowerment – to reach mutual agreement between different and equal employee voices, through open, straight and collaborative communication. Each employee had a personal responsibility to express her thoughts, feelings, and ideas, and to be sensitive to the emotions of others. This was not a perfect world, there were problems, but these ideals were worked upon every day. This process of what Ashcraft calls *relational sensemaking* is also, I suggest, an example of responsive responsibility in which differences are recognized, heard and built upon. It is a view of organizations as communities, in which language and ways of relating to each other are important.

embodying management

We've talked about the crucial nature of language, emotions and bodies in organizations, and how each is both gendered and becoming increasingly 'managed' in front stage performances, as part of cultural norms and performance management, and in the hyperreal. Emotional or *aesthetic labour*, where employees find their hearts, minds and bodies becoming a commodity in the economic contract of work, is a feature of contemporary work life – especially in the service industry. Yet as we have seen, it has personal costs, raising ethical dilemmas, emotional conflict and feelings of inauthenticity: Is this really who I am? Can I act the part and feel good about myself? There can also be organizational costs in that aesthetic labour diminishes spontaneity of feeling, genuine civility and concern, and can be perceived by customers as calculated manipulation. To what extent is it morally acceptable to require employees to *be* in a particular way – because this form of labour is not just a performance, but relates to identity, emotions and our sense of self.

Let's take this back to the various conceptualizations in Chapter 1 of who managers are. Are managers as rational agents expected to suppress or quash their emotions? Are managers as actors expected to manage and perform emotion according to role expectations? Are managers as subjectivities to be seen either as emotion-less or as sites for conflicting emotions? Managers are embodied people with feelings – which they express whether they are aware of it or not. They use phrases such as "I feel ...', 'I'm frustrated about ...', 'I was really angry when...' We are our bodies and our emotions – we don't leave them at the door when we go to work. As we have seen, scientific language and the rational techniques advocated in systematized and professionalized management Discourse do not capture much of what goes on in organizations. Antonio Strati (1999) argues that managers also need to recognize *sensible*, *sensory* or *aesthetic* forms of knowing through the body and through our emotions. This brings us into the realm of aesthetics, the idea that our 'experience of the real is first and foremost sensory experience of a physical reality' (Gagliardi, 1999: 311) – a *felt experience* he terms *pathos*. Gagliardi (1990) suggests that we experience organizations as aesthetically pleasing (as beautiful, sublime and gracious) and/or ugly (as grotesque, repugnant and painful). We may experience beauty and joy in the rhythm and flow of work or comedy in jokes and stories shared between colleagues. We've already seen examples of such felt experiences in managers' comments, and of the disconnect and tension that people feel when forced to perform emotion. Feelings we need to be sensitive to.

improvising

Finally, one developing area of interest of managers and academics, that can incorporate reflexive and responsive ways of managing is that of improvisation: we mentioned this briefly as part of managing meaning. It's an idea taken from the theatre and from jazz, and connected with strategy and innovation, organizational design and learning, problem solving, teamwork and managing performance.[8] Rational approaches to management emphasize the need for tight control through the application of techniques, to reduce instances where managers might be 'out of control' and forced to improvise. Managing meaning, authoring and reflexivity require a great deal of improvisation: responsiveness, being responsive and open to the possibilities of the moment, an ability to respond to discontinuity, complexity and the unanticipated.

Much of what we do in organizations is improvisation, a manager or team working on a problem with no well-defined answer or protocol: a customer requests something different, a machine breaks down for no apparent reason ... we improvise solutions, play it by ear and make it up as we go along in our everyday conversations and actions. Improvisation is more than creativity (which, ironically, has been routinized in the development of creative management techniques), it's an extemporaneous process that involves intuition, and what an ex-colleague of mine referred to as pedamentability, or thinking on your feet. If you want to see a good example of improvisation through creatively using all the resources to hand, watch the film *Apollo 13* when NASA is trying to figure out how to get the astronauts back to earth. Improvising means using knowledge and experience in new ways, by being sensitive to what's going on around you. Improvising is also implicit in relationally responsive interaction, because, as we have seen, much of our conversation involves responding in the moment.

Dusya Vera and Mary Crossan (2004) suggest that the process of improvisation means being in the moment: listening, creating the freedom to improvise, focusing on novelty and not being bound by rules, focusing on the process rather than the output, emphasizing spontaneity not judgement, using 'yes, and' to build on ideas rather than shoot them down, working collaboratively, and evaluating the process of improvisation through what Weick (1998) calls the aesthetics of imperfection (that is, saying 'okay, given the constraints and opportunities of the situation, then this is a creative outcome'). I would add that improvisation also means playing with 'what if ...?', exploring possibilities and different ways of thinking. Improvisation is spontaneous, risky, unpredictable, exciting, scary, and requires an acceptance that failure can happen but that we can learn from it. I suggest it requires polyphony and a truly relational stance. It means a shift in many organizations, creating a culture where improvisation is encouraged and supported, and managers are prepared to take and accept risks. And improvisation suggests that managers are *bricoleurs* – adept at crafting new ways of seeing and doing things from the myriad of resources around them: appreciating complexity, going beyond rules and procedures, encouraging multiple interpretations, engaging in relational and reflexive practice, creating new meanings and stories, and combining resources, knowledge and expertise in new ways.

summary

In this chapter we've built on the two key premises of the previous chapters, that managers need to reflexively interrogate taken-for-granted practices, and that there is a dialectical relationship between language and 'reality', to explore different ways of thinking about managing culture, power and authority, and the nature of management. In following these paths, we've found that management is not as straightforward as we might think, but often encompasses hidden meanings, practices and consequences. If we look at alternative readings (obversion), then managing organizational culture is not as benign a process as we might think; power and resistance can be seen as two sides of the same coin; we can think about responsibility as relational; and management as implicitly gendered. We explored ways in which employees may engage in resistance (subversion): linguistically, relationally and practically. And finally, if we accept the notion of polyphony – that organizations are communities of difference – then how can managers make a difference? I suggest that the answer lies not in minimizing difference, but recognizing and building on differences to manage people and organizations in more responsive and ethical ways. This involves a relational stance, in which managers recognize they are always in relation to others; are self reflexive about the impact of their assumptions and ways of speaking and relating; and are critically reflexive about the impact of managerial ideologies, and management discourse and practice.

notes

1   http://www.microsoft.com/uk/careers/values.mspx (accessed 19.9.2008).
2   See Borofsky (2005) for a discussion of the controversy and its implications.
3   *Wall Street Journal*, 20 February 2002.
4   Based on the 2007 UK Annual Survey of Hours and Earnings, data on the US afl-cio website, and the 2006 EOWA census in Australia.
5   http://warner.blogs.nytimes.com/2008/06/05/woman-in-charge-women-who-charge/?ex=1213502400&en=444e6325f8d5a3ed&ei=5070&emc=eta1.
6   See work by Ashcraft, Calas and Smircich, Collinson, and Marshall, and the journal *Gender, Work and Organization* for examples.
7   See Argyris (1991).
8   See *Organization Science* Special Issue (1998); Orlikowski and Hoffman (1997).

4

Managing Ethical and 'Just' Organizations

Ethical intention [is] *aiming at the 'good life' with and for others, in just institutions.*

Ricoeur, 1992: 172

I want to begin this final chapter by saying that I'm a moral optimist. I believe fundamentally that people are good and that we can live well together. Yes, we make mistakes and people are going to let you down. Yes, evil exists. Yes, managers and employees act in unethical and self-interested ways. And yes, organizations can be pathological in that conflict, alienation, discrimination, bullying and other inequities exist. But the point of this chapter is that if we don't believe we can act in morally good ways and create an organizational life characterized by ethical and just behaviour, then we are never going to change anything. The alternative readings of managing and managers that I've offered in previous chapters all lead up to the main point of this chapter: *That managers are responsible for managing in ethical and moral ways and for creating responsive, ethical and 'just' organizations.* This is the ultimate goal of Critical Management Studies, to advocate more humane, socially responsible and just forms of managing and organizing. So the purpose of this chapter is to explore what this might mean, and in particular to take Ricoeur's notion of ethical intention and relate it to managing organizations.

I draw on Ricoeur's work particularly because he views ethics and morality as both interpersonal and institutional, which means that each of us takes responsibility for acting in ethical ways as well as ensuring that equity, morality and justice exist at an organizational level. In other words, we have both a personal and an institutional responsibility. There's a danger when studying ethics, in looking purely at moral theory without embedding it in practice, or looking at a moral practice uninformed by theory. Canadian political and moral philosopher Charles Taylor argues that we need to examine the relationship between moral theory, common understandings and background practices. He uses the term *social imaginary* to describe the latter:

> something much broader and deeper than the intellectual schemes people may entertain when they think about social reality in a disengaged mode. I am thinking, rather, of the ways people imagine their social existence, how they fit together with others, how things go on between them and their fellows, the expectations that are normally met, and the deeper normative notions and images that underlie these expectations. (2004: 23)

I want to suggest that an understanding of our background practices – our relationally responsive interaction – is crucial to managing in ethical ways: *that we need to consider the moral social imaginaries within organizational life and the responsibilities these bring for managers.* This is where Ricoeur's ideas meet the idea of managing as a relational practice, and offer a way forward, for he believes ethics (being a good person) and morality (moral laws and the rule of justice) are interwoven.

We'll begin this chapter by looking at some of the current issues relating to business ethics, and then move on to explore Ricoeur's ideas and their implications for managing organizations in ethical and moral ways.

what is 'ethics'?

> *Ethics? I suppose the most common definition of ethics is the attempt to build a systematic set of normative prescriptions about human behaviour, codes to govern everyday morals and morality.*
>
> *Parker, 1998: 1*

There's a plethora of journal articles and books on ethics, including religious, philosophical, political, academic and professional texts. Yet despite this, or perhaps because of it, there is still much debate on what ethics is, should be and should do; about whether we can identify universal ethical norms; about whose ethical principles are the correct ones (as the saying goes, 'one person's terrorist is another person's freedom fighter'); and about whether ethical prescriptions influence practice. I discovered an article written in 1911 by George Adams, who argues that religion and metaphysics just aren't enough, because they define absolute ideals and truths rather than focus on common sense or practical life. He says that we need to be concerned with 'the humbler task of the organization of our social experience, the relief of poverty, the freeing of human life everywhere from the obstructions which greed and ignorance impose, – with acting everywhere in the light of ideals wholly relative to the best we know and can do' (p. 229). And I agree with him. Having moral ideals and laws in place is fine, but ethics is essentially about human behaviour and practical action: about how we treat each other in our everyday interactions in organizations and in society at large.

There are a number of major debates in philosophical ethics, one of which is that of moral universalism versus moral relativism. The meaning of these terms can be debated, so let me frame this debate as one between those who believe that morality is grounded in universal laws, values, principles and a system of ethics that apply to everyone everywhere (often equated with universalism), and those who believe that morality is grounded in the actual relationships we live out with one another (often equated with relativism). The former view relates to the idea that there are human rights fundamental to all people, regardless of where they live. The 1948 Universal Declaration of Human Rights addresses those rights; for example, Article 4 states that 'No one shall be held in slavery or servitude; slavery and the slave trade shall be prohibited in all their forms.' Those who believe morality is grounded in relationships claim that moral values are culturally influenced, and therefore moral judgements are subjective. If we place this debate within a business context, it is perhaps best illustrated by the issue of what constitutes bribery. In the USA, it's a crime to use money or other forms of payoffs to win business both at home and overseas. Yet what may be constituted as a bribe in one country might be seen as an accepted social norm of gift-giving in another. And to partly counter the difficulties associated with these differences, the WTO (World Trade Organization) and OECD (Organization for Economic Cooperation and Development) address international anti-bribery by establishing common agreements – conventions that are enforceable by law.

Another debate centres on the issue of whether ethical laws and prescriptions influence practice. Despite having laws and ethical codes of conduct, corruption, fraud and other forms of ethical misconduct are still prevalent in organizations. And this is often related to the behaviour of individual organizational members. Barings Bank and BCCI were brought down by rogue traders; Bernard Ebbers, the CEO of WorldCom was convicted for his part in an estimated $11 billion accounting fraud; Arthur Andersen, one of the Big Five Accounting Firms ceased auditing and went from 85,000 to 200 employees worldwide after being convicted of the obstruction of justice in relation to the Enron investigation – brought to public attention by the disclosure that two managers told employees to shred potentially incriminating documents. Yet Arthur Andersen had a reputation for upholding high ethical standards, and ran training sessions and conferences on ethics and anti-corruption as late as 2001.[1] Another well-known international company, Chevron Texaco, currently faces a $16 billion environmental lawsuit filed by Ecuadorian indigenous groups back in 1993; it paid $275 million to settle a lawsuit that charged the company with releasing 'extremely hazardous substances' into the air in the US; and in 1996 Chevron paid $115 million as a result of a class action suit regarding discrimination against African-American employees. A tape of Texaco executives making racial comments led to a national boycott of Texaco products. And the list of corporate malfeasance goes on …

So why aren't ethical codes of conduct and training enough? Is it that managing and ethics are a contradiction in terms? Is it a case of 'do as I say not as I do'? Or is there a conflict between what it means to be a good person, a good employee and a good manager – between personal and professional ethics, loyalty and morality? Employees face moral dilemmas every day. One example from my own experience comes to mind: I was instructed to carry out an act I knew was illegal under the threat of being ostracized because I was not being a 'team player'. I didn't comply, and it may be just coincidental that I was soon after passed over for promotion. Is it that we somehow don't get the balance right between universal ideals and individual responsibility? Robert Jackall's classic 1988 study of managerial life in corporate America, *Moral Mazes*, focuses on the moral rules-in-use managers employ in day-to-day operations. He argues that managers hold a pivotal institutional and social position because 'their occupational ethics and the way they come to see the world set both the frameworks and the vocabularies for a great many public issues in our society' (p. 12). Yet despite this position, he found managers were not subject to universal moral truths, rather needing to be alert to their organizational requirements and to expediency, the 'ideological idols of the moment' (p. 133). In doing so, they viewed relationships in a strictly utilitarian way, while continually assessing the moral fitness of their colleagues. He suggests that the moral action of managers is influenced by organizational criteria of 'success', by how one has to prove one's worth, and by the moral viewpoints and methodological rationalities of bureaucracies. In other words, managers are subject to moral relativism.

An argument for the failure of ethical codes of practice is that such codes can actually encourage employees to cheat, because they give the cheaters a competitive advantage over others. One example is whistle blowing, where in the US a person can file a Qui Tam lawsuit in the name of the US Government, claiming fraud by government contractors – and receive a share of the recovered money. One could take a cynical perspective and argue that the longer the whistleblower keeps quiet before reporting any such activity – the bigger the payout. And the UK government is currently (summer 2008) considering a similar law. This argument about encouraging cheating also relates to industry codes and international agreements, which depend on all organizations sticking to the agreement. The violation of a code, let's say anti-bribery, by one organization can give that organization a huge competitive advantage. So opposing pressures can exist for both conformity and nonconformity, and it's important to consider what those might be and to try to anticipate and minimize the counter pressures to ethical action. *Moral communities are created by the beliefs, values, actions and commitments of individual members of that moral community.*

Furthermore, as we saw in Chapter 1, the various conceptualizations of managers have implications for how we view ethics. For example, rational managers will probably work from an enlightened perspective by engaging in objective moral reflection and reasoned action to the benefit of the 'common' good. But as we have seen, what constitutes rationality and the common good is open to interpretation and is a political process based on self and/or group interests. Managers as actors may engage in performances that have ethical implications because they are aimed at manipulating other actors or other performances. If we see managers as discursively constructed subjects then we will recognize the danger of taking power for granted and the inequities that can occur as particular subjects become marginalized – subjects who may have no opportunity to resist or to change the situation. Critically reflexive managers identify power inequalities and marginalization, but also have to consider that they act within broader communities who may not hold similar ideals or norms.

This brings us to the notion of ethical and unethical organization cultures – however we might view 'culture'. Stan Deetz, Sarah Tracy and Jennifer Simpson (2000) identify six cultural elements conducive to unethical behaviour in organizations:

- Closed, highly cohesive work groups where members are unwilling to question facts or decisions and to present alternative viewpoints.
- Vision statements written in vague ways that are open to interpretation and can lead to contradictory and unintended outcomes.
- Too many hierarchical levels or departments, which can result in commitment to one's peers and impede communication and collaboration.
- Incentive programmes that encourage competition and self-interest.
- Organizational practices, norms, and rituals that discriminate and privilege particular groups in intended and unintended ways.
- Policies and practices that lead to codes of silence, where employees feel pressured to act in unethical ways or feel unable to discuss ethical dilemmas or report unethical behaviour.

Enron is a good example of just such an unethical culture. Enron had a code of ethics that listed 'Principles of Human Rights'. So what went wrong? As a *Time* magazine article stated in February 2002 after the company filed Chapter 11 bankruptcy:

> It was Skilling [the CEO] who provided the strategic vision behind Enron, who transformed its old gas-pipeline culture into a swaggering,

rule-breaking, dealmaking cult that ultimately mislaid its analytical skills and perhaps its moral compass. Skilling, a Harvard M.B.A. and former McKinsey & Co. consultant, had a high-wattage intellect that always impressed. Even when he was a student, people who met him knew he would do something big.[2]

They perhaps didn't realize how big! Skilling was convicted for fraud, conspiracy, insider trading and lying to auditors, and was sentenced to 24 years in jail in 2006. The Enron corporate 'cult'ure was one of 'creative' accounting, aggressive risk-taking, and a feeling of invulnerability, where subsidiary companies were established with names inspired by *Star Wars* and *Jurassic Park* characters such as Raptor and Chewco. Imagine how difficult it was to go against the norm. It required moral courage to be the one person to defy orders, or question unethical and (in this case) illegal action. Culture can become a cult, good or bad. The Enron case reinforces the crucial role that senior managers play in creating and maintaining an ethical culture.

This sounds all too pessimistic. But what it serves to do is highlight that organizational ethics are complex and are, as Robert Jackall says, moral mazes with multidimensional aspects, competing pressures and various interpretations of what might be reasonable and ethical depending on whose point of view. The classic example of a moral maze can be seen in the 1987 *Challenger* Space Shuttle disaster, and the various pressures experienced by Morton-Thiokol managers and engineers during a 1987 teleconference with NASA and the Marshall Space Flight Center about whether it was safe to launch. After recommending not to launch the shuttle at temperatures below 53 degrees Fahrenheit, Morton-Thiokol senior managers and engineers had an off-line discussion, feeling under pressure by NASA to justify their decision with data they couldn't produce. At one point, the General Manager said, 'Take off your engineering hat and put on your management hat.' This simple statement reframed the issues under consideration from a technical decision to a political one of meeting customer requirements, and changed the vote to a recommendation to launch with no additional technical data.[3] It illustrates both the power of language and the importance of taking a moral stance.

Can we take anything from the literature and from business experience that might be helpful in managing organizations in ethical and socially responsible ways?

ethics and management

Today, business ethics is part of most management education programmes, and is a legitimate concern of both research and practice. As a topic of study, business ethics addresses a number of issues, including the ethical nature of capitalism, the ability of business ethics to impact on business practice, the challenges of meeting all stakeholder demands in responsible and ethical ways, corporate governance practices, and the role of moral reflection and debate. Three issues stand out:

corporate social responsibility (CSR)

CSR addresses such concerns as environmental pollution, global warming, worldwide poverty, child labour, community sustainability and politically correct accounting/marketing. A number of organizations identify core CSR values. The UK-based Co-operative Bank is currently running TV adverts stating that they do not invest in oppressive regimes or businesses who supply arms, and that they refuse loans to companies who act in conflict with the Co-op's ethical policy. Ben & Jerry's, the Vermont-based Ice Cream Company have a list of core values based on the interests of the original founders of the company. These include:

- We strive to create economic opportunities for those who have been denied them and to advance new models of economic justice that are sustainable and replicable.
- We support sustainable and safe methods of food production that reduce environmental degradation, maintain the productivity of the land over time, and support the economic viability of family farms and rural communities.
- We strive to show a deep respect for human beings inside and outside our company and for the communities in which they live.[4]

CSR recognizes an issue we discussed in Chapter 1, the pivotal role managers and organizations play in society today, and a manager's responsibility to the community at large.

business ethics

A second issue is *business ethics,* which focuses on the development of codes of ethics and ethical frameworks relating to workplace issues and employer–employee relationships. Over the last 10 years, business ethics has become part of many management education programmes, and often draws on philosophy, contrasting the utilitarian ethics of Hobbes (1651), Bentham (1789) and Mill (1861) with the duty ethics of Kant (1785) and Rawls (1971). While utilitarian ethics advocates that the enlightened and educated mind judges actions by their consequences, for example, as Bentham argued, the greatest good/happiness for the greatest number, duty ethics focuses on the inherent rightness and wrongness of actions and the motivation behind such actions and decisions. In order to make a point while risking oversimplification, utilitarian ethics is perhaps best (although ironically!) captured in the notion that *ethics pays.* In other words, that being seen to be ethical both looks good and is good for business because it maximizes profit – which ultimately benefits everyone. This instrumental notion of ethics encourages conformity and obedience rather than a reflexive questioning of the fundamental responsibilities of business and the wider social impact of managerial decision making. Indeed, as Hugh Willmott (1998) says, it can be seen as just another way of controlling employee behaviour towards organizational values and interests.

Within duty ethics, Immanuel Kant argued that we understand our experience through innate knowledge that helps us organize what's happening around us. He assumed that morality is related to rational beings accepting and acting upon universal law, and argued that we should act out of respect for moral law rather than self-interest – and a moral law is good if it is able to withstand contradiction. His famous dictum – 'Always treat humanity, whether in yourself or in other people, as an end in itself and never as a mere means' – still stands the test of time today. John Rawls offers a good example of moral universalism because he provides a theory of justice that says a moral law can be valid if generalized to everyone, and to do so we have to use what he calls an imaginative device – to put ourselves in a neutral position behind a veil of ignorance, then to imagine what a 'just' world would look like. This gives a basis for articulating what is 'just', and for providing criteria against which we measure existing institutions. To do so, Rawls argues that we need to completely abstract ourselves from the actual social world – a totally opposite view to that of Charles Taylor's social imaginaries, which emphasizes an implicit grasp, or sense of moral order lying within our everyday practice. And, as I have asked in previous chapters, when can we ever be neutral? Neutrality and abstraction imply a god-like being, with no history or biography, someone who exists outside a social context with his/her own particular ways of thinking and acting ... and I haven't met anyone like that! But an absence of neutrality shouldn't surely prevent managers from working within the polyphony of social experience, recognizing that there are different views but that we can sit down and come to some agreement about what a 'just' organization should be?

ethical leadership

Ethical leadership defines and examines the core principles and virtues central to ethical and more democratic management of organizations. A major aspect of this work is virtue ethics, which goes back to Aristotle and Plato, who argued that ethics relates to the character and motives of people: we do what is right because we are virtuous. Virtue ethics is about living our lives in purposeful and virtuous ways. For Aristotle, this meant achieving phronesis, the practical wisdom or prudence necessary to enhance our happiness and quality of life. A number of well-known leaders are hailed for their philanthropy. Bill Gates, co-founder of Microsoft, established the Bill and Melinda Gates Foundation in 2000, with a $27 billion endowment dedicated to reducing inequities around the world. But philanthropy and leadership also exist at the local level. For example, one large car dealership in New Mexico has a free on-site nurse and 24-hour clinic for employees and their families, and is one of the few car dealerships that is closed on Sunday because of the owner's view that Sunday is family time. For the owner, this is not a question of profit, but of 'running my business the right way'. A number of senior managers I know talk about the importance of having a person within and outside of the organization who will listen, question and act as a moral compass for them. Someone who, as one manager commented:

> holds me accountable for my actions, and also challenges my thinking in a way that no one else has ever done before. He models for me the

value of servant-leadership and also integrity in character. He tries to stretch me beyond myself, beyond my normal methods of operating and thinking, by challenging my assumptions.

feminist ethics

Over the last 15 years, feminist ethics have offered an alternative way of thinking about ethics and management. Lawrence Kohlberg (1969), whose work was initially based on Rawls' theory of justice, identified six stages of moral reasoning through which he believed we must move if we are to become more morally and socially responsible. His work is often used in business ethics programmes to teach students how to become moral agents. In *In A Different Voice*, Carol Gilligan (1982) argued that Kohlberg's work was gender biased because his studies were only of men, and he assumed that the moral thinking of males would be representative of all humanity. Men scored higher on questionnaires relating to the model, and Kohlberg argued that women were lower on the scale of moral development than men because they didn't move past Stage 3 of the model. Gilligan suggested that the moral reasoning of women is different from men in that women emphasize care, trust, mutuality and responsibility, in other words, relationships rather than rights and justice. So rather than working from a morality of justice based on the injunction not to hurt others, women work from a morality of care, which means acting responsively to others.

Even though Gilligan is careful to argue that both are valid modes of understanding, her work has been criticized by some feminist scholars such as Judith Butler, who argue that feminist ethics reinforce the gender stereotyping and oppression of women as underpaid carers, and emphasize the division between public (organizational) and private (caring family) life. Nevertheless, Gilligan's work has been instrumental in drawing attention to the care-less use of one voice – the patriarchal voice – that's so pervasive and powerful in the realm of theory and practice. And she shifted attention from an abstract, universal and dispassionate consideration of individual rights and ethics, to a relational voice and connectedness – the need to consider our primary ethical responsibility for others in actual circumstances. Whether we agree or disagree that the moralities of justice and care follow gender demarcation, her belief that a sensitivity to human relationships is central to moral understanding is an important way of viewing the ethical responsibilities of managers. And a relational voice takes on very practical connotations through the following evocative comment:[5]

> Listening to human voices, Noel finds that one voice, speaking in a particular emotional register can stop the emotional vibrations in a group of people so that the environment in the room becomes deadened or flat. When this happens, she observes, it looks like silence but in fact the feelings and thoughts – the psychological energy – often move into the only place they can still live, and vibrate in silence, in the inner sense, until it becomes possible to bring them back into the world... (Gilligan, 1995: 121)

Have you ever sat in a meeting and felt the 'deadening' of the conversation after someone speaks? Where, based on what one person has said or how they've said it, other participants feel that their voice will not be heard and so remain silent? In this instance, dialogue becomes a monologue. This has real implications for the way we interact and relate with others in personal and organizational settings.

A feminist ethics of care plays through Joan Acker's notion of the non-responsibility of work organizations. She argues that within western society, economic organizations are privileged over other forms of life. Many organizations are characterized by non-responsibility, 'refusals or attempts to avoid contributions to meeting the needs of people, if these contributions do not directly enhance production or accumulation' (2005: 94). She frames her argument by saying that economic activity is about the processes of *provisioning* – providing the necessities of community and survival through reproduction – and *production*, which is about profit. In capitalist societies, the focus is on the latter, on rational economic man and the rational manager. The production process is not just one of unequal power, it's gendered (because women are mainly involved in provisioning and in the unpaid work of caring and reproduction), racialized (racial and ethnic minorities often occupy low-paid, menial jobs), and class-based because working class jobs often don't incorporate provisioning needs. This leads to what she calls the non-responsibility of capitalist organizations for meeting the provisioning needs of society, particularly in relation to issues of minimum wage, pay equity, benefits, quality day care, family leave, work/life balance, product safety, and environmental and community responsibility.

Businesses often do not consider or act on these issues until forced to by legislation and, as Acker says, the ideal employee is often seen to be the person without family or community obligations. Employees often face career choices in which the work expectations associated with advancement have serious consequences for life outside work. And while this has negative consequences for both men and women, women are mainly affected because they are traditionally responsible for caring. Acker suggests that we need to redefine the process of production and the organization of work to value and support both work and family. Of course, many businesses resist this because they think it has a negative impact on profitability. But would you be committed to, and want to stay with, an organization that requires you to work 60 hours a week with below minimum pay? Should employers have a duty of care for the mental and physical health of their employees? Sweden, for example, has generous parental leave benefits: 240 days per parent, of which 80 per cent are paid, flexible work arrangements, and sabbatical leave for employees.

can managers be ethical?

There is debate around whether management and ethics are a contradiction in terms. The cynics argue that management, ethics and morality don't go together because managers have to act on behalf of owners and shareholders rather than the common good. So, in the interest of efficiency and profit, managers have to view people as instrumental – objects or assets to be manipulated like any other material resource. Moral and political philosopher Alasdair MacIntyre, whose work explores the relationship between morality, culture and politics, argues this view eloquently. A central theme in his work is that modern life lacks a moral code and civility, and that this needs to change. In his 1981 book *After Virtue*, he considers the moral inconsistencies within society, about how we often justify our actions and preferences by using the language of reason and morality. Two particular issues are relevant to our discussion of management.

First, MacIntyre argues controversially that morality in today's world is characterized by emotivism, the idea that moral judgements are not based on universal criteria but are expressions of preference and self-interest in which we try to obtain our goals by persuasion and by emotional appeals. Thus, we are always trying to gain power over others – just as they are trying to gain power over us. Does this mean that people who are good at manipulating others, who desire power, who are self-interested and who treat people as means not ends, are those who become leaders? MacIntyre believes so, for as he famously declares, the barbarians have been governing us for some time (p. 263)! And if this is so, what does this mean for civilized and 'just' organizations?

Second, he describes managers as 'characters', representatives of modern culture and its moral ideals. Characters are clusters of moral beliefs, activities and attitudes that legitimate a way of being and acting. For MacIntyre, the problem lies in the idea that managers are perceived as engaging in value-neutral activities that are concerned with rational and efficient means rather than ends. This is reinforced through language that frames people as objects: as assets, costs and benefits. As a result, people are ignored, as managers (knowingly or otherwise) manipulate others to achieve organizational goals. The irony lies in our seeing ourselves as moral agents: we think we are autonomous, free, that there are self evident truths, and that we do not manipulate others, nor are we manipulated by them. But we do and are! He argues that managers justify their authority by claiming they have the skills and expertise to make the organization effective and efficient. But, he asks, 'What if effectiveness is part of a masquerade of social control rather than a reality?' ... because the kind of knowledge that sustains such expertise is 'one more moral fiction' (p. 75).

The managers in Robert Jackall's study in a way recognized this fiction: one former Vice President in the study commented, *'What is right in the corporation is what the guy above you wants from you. That's what morality is in the corporation'* (1988: 6). Executive and business school programmes offering more efficient ways of achieving organizational goals maintain this moral fiction by teaching rational management techniques and egocentric and heroic approaches to leadership which focus on confident action rather than a moral debate on goals or social responsibility. A critical evaluation of ends is generally not part of the curriculum. Managers are exhorted 'To boldly go where no man has gone before' – as embodied in the famously declared *Star Trek Enterprise* mission statement (of course we can contrast this 1960s Captain Kirk heroic style with Captain Picard's more cerebral and collaborative approach). As Sumantra Ghoshal states, 'By propagating ideologically inspired amoral theories, business schools have actively freed their students from any sense of moral responsibility' (2005: 76). If we frame ethics as part of this moral fiction of rationality and neutrality, then we should be able to develop an ethical algorithm that eliminates moral debate and gives us a logical answer to any ethical dilemma … and such algorithms do exist!

I've found that MacIntyre's ideas about management often cause much debate, and sometimes denial, among students – but consider a comment made by a manager in my class a few years ago:

> My initial role was that of an operations analysis manager. In simpler terms I performed statistical analysis and mathematical modeling to justify the Assistant General Manager's decisions to reduce workforce and require his management staff to do more with less. In this role I was the essence of bureaucratic rationality, 'the rationality of matching means to ends economically and efficiently' (MacIntyre, 1981: 25). Further I can honestly confess that consistent to the character of a manager described by MacIntyre, I was not 'engaged in moral debate'. My work was used directly in justifying over 300 layoffs and countless sleepless nights for other managers who had to figure out how to deliver on ever increasing service standards, with higher revenue and transactions, while having less labor. While performing this I never concerned myself with the moral implications of such work, rather I took great pride in 'technique, with effectiveness in transforming … investment into profits' (Ibid., p. 30).

This is part of the taken-for-granted nature of management that we discussed in previous chapters, and of the idea that managers themselves are victims of the logic of managerialism: subject to the pressures to produce and to act 'rationally', and be rewarded for doing so.

Increasingly, managers are the victims and not just the agents of a rationality that inhibits critical reflection upon, and transformation of, a structure of social relations that systematically impedes and distorts efforts to develop more ethically rational, morally defensible forms of management theory and practice. (Alvesson and Willmott, 1996: 36)

This all sounds rather cynical, overly critical, and depressing. Are managers really just morally neutral technicians? Do managers engage in moral debate? Are organizations doomed to be pathological or can they be different? These questions highlight the moral complexities of organizational life. As individuals, we face moral choices because 'what is right' is interpreted in various ways, and in organizations we find ourselves coping with many different pressures and having to answer to various 'stakeholders' – but ultimately to ourselves. This is where I turn to phenomenology and Ricoeur's work ...

moral managers

phenomenology and ethics

Existentialism's first move is to make every man aware of what he is and to make the full responsibility of his existence rest on him. And when we say that a man is responsible for himself, we do not only mean that he is responsible for his own individuality, but that he is responsible for all men.

Sartre, 1965: 36

We began this book by drawing on a philosophical understanding, and I'm returning to philosophy in this final chapter. While there's a general assumption that philosophy is about very abstract and esoteric issues, there are many aspects that address serious and practical issues about the way we live our lives. Philosophy, and in particular phenomenology, speak to ethics because they give us a context in which to situate and question our beliefs about the way the world works, about the nature of knowledge, and about who we are. They also, as in the quote by Sartre above, address our responsibility for others. And while most managers ordinarily don't have time to sit down and read philosophical texts, I've found that when they do, they find some intriguing and useful ideas. Let me set the scene by sketching the main concerns of phenomenology.

Phenomenology explores the relationship between ourselves and our lived experience, or, in phenomenological terms, our *life-world*. We can trace its roots back to the work of Husserl, Sartre, Heidegger and to some of the authors we've mentioned previously, namely Merleau-Ponty and Ricoeur. Although there are different approaches to phenomenology, the unifying theme is a concern about viewing the world in terms of 'things' and objects: as abstract representations such as systems, models, laws and categories. For phenomenologists, objects and events only gain meaning as we encounter them in human consciousness; they do not have meaning independent of our perception. If we look back to Chapter 1 at the various ways in which managerial identity has been theorized, you may note it has most frequently been framed in generalized object-oriented ways, for example managers as rational agents, actors or discursive subjects. Think about management and leadership courses you may have attended where you have completed self-assessment and personality questionnaires to discover what type of manager or leader you are. Such instruments provide generalized social categories such as introvert/ extrovert, people or task oriented, transformative or transactional, etc., against which we can compare ourselves. And here lies a fundamental issue, because phenomenologists, in particular Sartre, Merleau-Ponty and Ricoeur, suggest that thinking about ourselves purely in terms of such external referents and general social categories strips us of our humanness, and turns us into objects separate from our everyday lived experience. Thinking about ourselves as a 'what' (as 'the management', 'a rational manager', an 'introvert') removes any sense of responsibility for our actions and for our relationships with others. We take these categorizations for granted and we don't engage in a critical questioning of our actions.

Briefly, Husserl's work on transcendental phenomenology was concerned with how the world appears to us through our perception or imagination; with studying the true nature or *essence* of something by *bracketing experience*, for example examining the structure and properties of consciousness while suspending questions and beliefs about the nature of the world.[6] So Husserl's phenomenology involved studying how we come to know phenomena (objects and events) through a disembodied consciousness. His ideas provided inspiration for a number of scholars, who went on to develop variations of phenomenology, including Sartre, whose work is often regarded as the cornerstone of *existential phenomenology*, and Ricoeur, who developed an approach to phenomenology he called *hermeneutic phenomenology*.

Existential phenomenologists such as Sartre and Heidegger are more concerned with the nature of being *in the lived world*. Sartre (1956) for example, suggests that *Being* is becoming, that human nature isn't fixed: at first we are nothing and we make ourselves who we are by imagining who we will be. Thus, we are 'condemned to be free' (p. 529) because we are responsible for making choices about who we are and what to do – and in those choices lie both uncertainties and opportunities to realize our being. An awareness of these opportunities and possibilities constitutes one aspect of *being*, that is *being-for-itself* – a self-conscious reflective person. A second aspect, *being-in-itself*, Sartre claims just *is* – is our lives, who we are, pre-conscious and acting instinctively. A third aspect is that of *non-being* or *nothingness*. Sartre captures the relationship between being and nothingness when he argues that I am not the self I will be, because there are infinite possibilities and choices in between who I am and who I will become. Who we are will always be open because we are both pre-reflectively and self-reflectively embedded in the phenomenological moment of experience. What this means is that our personal and work identities are fluid. We are constantly expressing and figuring out who we are in our everyday experience as we interact with others and make choices about what to do.

But I believe it's hermeneutic phenomenology that offers a number of connections and insights for managers and leaders, because this version of phenomenology addresses issues of relationality, identity, critical reflection and ethics (Cunliffe, 2009). Not only is identity reflective and fluid, as Sartre suggests, but it's also socially embedded. Hermeneutics is about interpretation, and hermeneutic phenomenology addresses the interpretive nature of experience, identity and awareness. Ricoeur captures this succinctly when he says that our lives and our selves are an 'unending work of interpretation' (1992: 179) as we try to make sense of who we are and what's happening around us in order to make choices and act. Both Merleau-Ponty (1962, 1964) and Ricoeur argue that we cannot put aside, *bracket*, our surroundings, nor can we focus purely on the individual, because we are intersubjective and embodied beings. So whereas Sartre focused on being as a reflective self-conscious individual (an 'I'), Ricoeur and Merleau-Ponty believe we are inseparable from others ('We') and, particularly for Ricoeur, moral selves embracing the ethical intention of living a good life with others. This is where his work becomes relevant to managing ethical organizations.

For Ricoeur, knowing ourselves means asking the question 'Who am I in relation to others?', and this plays out in our everyday interaction. So we figure out who we are through interpretation and relationality, not purely through social categorization. You may see some connections here with Gilligan's notion of the relational voice. But for Ricoeur and Merleau-Ponty relationality, or in their terminology intersubjectivity, is not about two individuals coordinating their actions and coming to an understanding of what the other person thinks – indeed, this would take us back to the traditional communication model in Figure 1. Rather, I am who I am because of you – we are inseparable from others because whole parts of our life are part of their life history. Everything we say, think and do is interwoven with particular and generalized others: friends, colleagues, social and professional groups, categories, language systems, culturally and historically situated discursive and non-discursive practices. The *other* is always intertwined with us because we act in a complex web of present and previous relationships, conversations, utterances, language communities, speech genres and historical and cultural ways of speaking (Bakhtin, 1984, 1986). As we saw in Chapter 2, relationality is inherently practical, occurring in our everyday conversations and relationally responsive interaction, in which everything we do is a complex mixture of our own and others' actions and talk. In these living conversations we are inherently responsive to each other – to our own and others' words, gestures, and feelings. Our talk is so interwoven, that in our moment-by-moment dialogue, no one person is in control. This way of seeing the world means we have a moral responsibility to make available communicative opportunities to talk with, listen to, and be responsive to others. It also means we focus on collaborative forms of interacting: on dialogue not monologue, on creating shared meaning between us as we talk, rather than one person persuading the other that their way is the right one.

▇▇▇ who we are as managers: our ethical responsibility

Okay, so where does this take us in terms of managing organizations in ethical and responsive ways? Summarizing the main themes we've discussed up to this point:

- Codes of ethics only go so far – ethics is about our relationships with others, about how we act and treat others, both particular persons and the wider community.
- Managers are victims of the taken-for-granted notion that rationality, effectiveness and efficiency are neutral concepts, which legitimate their authority – when such concepts and practices are ideologically saturated.
- Generalizations and objectifications of self (the 'what') are useful up to a certain point, but can absolve us from ethical responsibility. Discovering 'who' we are can take us towards ethical relationships.
- Ethical action is not about one voice, but recognizing different voices and our responsibility for those voices.
- Ricoeur offers a way for us to think about how we might manage people in ethical ways and create ethical and moral organizations.

Of course, the question is: *How?*

In *Oneself as Another* (1992), Ricoeur builds on his earlier work on narrative, interpretation and ethics to explore three key issues. The first is how we can think about identity without losing a sense of self, or who we are, in the process. The second is the relationship between self and ethical intention. The third is how ethical selfhood relates to our broader social and institutional context. What he ends up with is a sort of moral philosophy and moral sociality, because he addresses how moral values and rules play through our relationships and the way we live our lives with others. As in the quote at the beginning of this chapter, he sees ethical intention as '*aiming at the "good life" with and for others, in just institutions*' (p. 172). How so? Bear with me a while here – we are going to look at some fairly complex philosophical ideas, but these ideas offer a different way of 'doing' ethics, by offering a way of thinking about how to 'be' ethical. Which resonates with one of the main premises of this book that if we know who we are or who to be – then what to do falls into place. The ideas have some very practical implications for managing organizations. I hope Ricoeurian scholars will forgive my distillation of his complex and nuanced work. Figure 4 offers an overview of the ideas we are going to discuss.

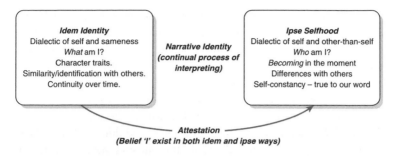

Figure 4   Narrative identity
Source: After Ricoeur, 1992

Ricoeur suggests we need to consider two modes of being: *idem* identity, that is, concerned with *what* we are; and *ipse* selfhood, that is, concerned with *who* we are. *Idem* is a Latin term meaning 'the same', so in this sense our identity revolves around how we see ourselves being similar to or the same as others. Sameness is often imputed by generalized character traits (such as introvert, neurotic, emotive) connecting us to others and offering continuity over time and contexts. Ricoeur sees these character traits as the 'what' of identity, because thinking about ourselves in terms of generalized physical and psychological characteristics turns us into an objectified person, or an individual at large: a combination of physical, mental and social predicates. Ricoeur says this is a 'portrait painted from outside' (1992: 119) and subjects us to already established categories, structures and mechanisms. We can think about the implications of *idem* identity if we go back to some of the conceptualizations of the role of a manager. If I think about myself as a manager in terms of being a figurehead, monitor, disturbance handler, etc. (Mintzberg, 1973 – see Table 1), then I will focus on those actions without necessarily questioning what this means or what the implications might be. There are also often ideal types associated with these generalized character traits, which can have an impact on what we do. For example, let's say you do a personality questionnaire and score highly as a neurotic introvert, does that explain who you are, and mean that because studies have shown good managers have low scores on neuroticism and are extroverts that you are never going to hack it as a manager? If you think about managers you know and respect, they are not going to have the same personality characteristics. These models are also gender and culturally biased – for example women score higher on neuroticism. The problem is that we often take *idem* conceptualizations as givens. And in so doing, we design hiring, performance appraisal, promotion and training programmes around such givens. So there are problems if we think purely in *idem* terms.

Ricoeur suggests we also need to consider *ipseity*, *ipse* being Latin for self. Ipseity is 'who' we are, our individual self and how we engage with the world. *Ipse* is how we are both the same as and different from others, about our uniqueness as an individuals. Ricoeur says that *ipse* emerges in the moments in which we open ourselves to others and find (intuitively and/or explicitly) how we are both similar to and different from others. For Ricoeur, both *idem* and *ipse* come together in our everyday interactions as we 'narrate' our sense of identity. What this means practically is that we interpret what is going on, what people are doing and who they are – including ourselves – and we try to create a coherent story about our experience and about what to do. So we create our narrative identity, an identity that both connects us to, and separates us from, others.

The final piece of the 'identity' puzzle is the notion of *attestation*. Ricoeur says attestation is my ability to see myself as a person in the narrative I'm creating (remember Merleau-Ponty's human dialectic from Chapter 1, the idea that we create the very social realities we think exist separately from us). Attestation means believing that I judge and act well, that I have an ethical intention to lead a good life, and that I can account for myself and my actions to others with conviction. But this does not mean being arrogant enough to believe that everything I do is right. Ethical selfhood involves an 'uneasy balance between attestation and suspicion' (Ricoeur, 1992: 302) – a balance between believing in myself and questioning myself. In practical terms this is about being self reflexive. Ricoeur says this means asking:

- Who is speaking?
- Who is acting?
- Who is interpreting?
- How does who I am as a moral person relate to my social surroundings and the moral norms?

In other words, we must question whether we are speaking and acting in ethical ways, and testing our illusions about ourselves and the meanings of our intentions (p. 240).

A useful way of thinking about this is an idea developed by Chris Argyris and Donald Schön (1974) who talk about the difference between our *espoused theories* (what we say) and our *theories-in-use* (what we do). They make the case that the two should be congruent. However, when asked about how we do something, we give our espoused theory, but the way we actually behave can be very different. I used to run one-day management seminars, where participants would say they definitely used participative approaches, but more often than not their immediate response to a short case study about a 'problematic' employee was to fire the person! You might want to check out Argyris's (1991) article, 'Teaching smart people how to learn', where he expands on defensive reasoning in organizations.

Ironically, as I'm writing this, one of my students has sent me a link to a webcast, which includes a video of US politician John Edwards. Edwards has just been in the news because of his alleged affair with the video's director.[7] The video begins by Edwards saying that he wants the American public to know 'who I really am', and shows him at a political rally saying, 'If we want to live in a moral, honest and just America, if we want to live in a moral and just world, we can't wait for somebody else to do it. *We* have to do it' – a disconnect between his espoused theory and his theory-in-use! It's interesting that he later says, 'We are conditioned to be political.' Regardless of your politics, the video is a not-to-be-missed example of impression management!

This example also brings us to Ricoeur's notion of ethical intention, which is the core of ethical selfhood because it's at the heart of who we are. He draws upon, and extends Aristotle's notion of phronesis, the practical wisdom necessary to enhance our happiness and quality of life, arguing that self and moral character are the cornerstones of ethics, as opposed to a moral society and moral norms. My interpretation of this point is that practical wisdom is a common sense and understanding that allows us to make ethical decisions in practical circumstances, without resorting only to universal laws or only to total relativism. And ethical selfhood means:

1 Self-constancy: being true to our word, being capable of evaluating our actions and believing they are ethical and good, and conducting ourselves so others may count on us. As he says: '"From you," says the other, "I expect you will keep your word"; to you, I reply: "You can count on me"' (1992: 286).

2   Solicitude: respecting others and their uniqueness as I respect myself. Viewing other people as irreplaceable and caring about them. This is not just friendship, but recognizing the suffering of others.
3   Self-esteem: which is the wish to live a good life, to esteem ourselves and others. This is the aim of an ethical life.
4   Reciprocity: where one hears and responds to others. Reciprocity involves dignity and respecting others for who they are.
5   Living well with others: which involves both interpersonal relations and justice and equality within institutions.

And, as you may see, ethical selfhood is different from *idem* identity because it's not about how we are the same as others, but about how we are the same over time (self-constant and true to our word) and how we respect our differences with others. So we experience the possibilities of who we are in relational moments of solicitude, reciprocity, and self-constancy. In practical terms this involves establishing relationships of mutual respect, appreciation and in creating good energy to work together.

Ethical selfhood is not about managing relationships, neither is it about blaming the situation as being at fault, it *is* about recognizing that we have a moral and social responsibility to understand what we can, and should, expect of ourselves and others. Ricoeur believes we have a personal responsibility for ethical action, and because we are always in relation to others, we have a duty of care to them. Thus, it's important for managers to consider *how* they relate to others; what assumptions they hold about people; to understand how others may view the world; and to create opportunities for open dialogue. This is an interpersonal ethics of managing, based on understanding who I am as a manager. It's a relational ethics which places responsibility for ethical ways of being and ethical action on myself. *Who I am in relation to others is important!*

managing 'just' and moral institutions

Ricoeur's work also connects with ethics and managing moral organizations because he is concerned with what 'just' institutions might look like. Whereas ethics is about aiming for the good life, morality is about moral norms and justice, and justice is about equality and what is legal. He rejects a foundational or universal view of ethics – the

Kantian idea of objective and universal moral laws, saying that ethics is 'enriched by the passage through the norm and exercising moral judgment in a given situation' (1992: 203). In other words, we need moral norms, but both they, and we as moral agents, are situated within a history and a social context that should not be ignored.

He also argues that conflict is unavoidable in moral life because of 'the agonistic ground of human experience' (p. 243); the differences that exist between old and young, society and individuals, male and female, and so on. Conflict also occurs within institutions because of different views about what is a 'just distribution' of goods, responsibilities, rights, etc.; different views about what is good government, and over how government or, more specifically, democracy is legitimized. You can perhaps begin to see the links with managing organizations. Ricoeur's work asks us to recognize that organizations are a play of voices, connected by a bond of common practices and customs rather than rules, in which each individual has a responsibility to herself or himself, as well as to other organizational members, to act in ethical and moral ways. Ricoeur doesn't ignore the dark side – he acknowledges that evil exists and that we do violence to each other in various intended and unintended ways. But he calls on us to recognize our responsibility *not* to do violence to others.

Violence might seem like a strong word to use, for it implies aggression, bullying, sexual harassment and verbal abuse, all of which occur in organizations. But violence can also take more insidious forms. Marie-France Hirigoyen (2005), talks about moral harassment – emotional violence caused by behaviour, words, facial expressions and gestures that degrade others. Neglect, ignoring employees by not giving them training or work assignment opportunities for example, and inaction can also be forms of violence, the latter in the sense that not acting against such behaviours can be seen as a form of complicity. Stephen Linstead addresses this issue in discussing organizational bystanding, 'where we know and may even witness the sort of injustice or bullying entailed by moral harassment, but do nothing about it' (2006: 208). He argues this can take three forms: ignoring what's happening around us; seeing injustice or moral harassment but failing to recognize it as such; or recognizing injustice or moral harassment and refusing to act, for whatever reason.

For Ricoeur, solicitude is crucial at the interpersonal and the institutional level. In the latter he defines solicitude as a concern for others through justice. To encapsulate his complex discussion of morality, he argues that just institutions are about the exercise of moral judgement and about *taking part* or deliberating well (1992: 247), which is tied in with power. Ricoeur talks about three forms of power: power over, power-to-do, and power-in-common. *Power over* is a form of violence exerted over others, including deceit (self-deceit and deceiving others), manipulation, domination and physical violence, which destroy respect and lead to suffering. Hierarchical organizations embody this form of power in many ways, not just in terms of managerial authority, but through the more insidious forms of power we discussed in Chapter 3. *Power-to-do* is the power to act and to be able to see myself as the author of my action. This isn't formal power as we typically think about it, but knowing that I can shape my experience and myself in my everyday actions and interactions – in other words managers as practical authors and reflexive practitioners. *Power-in-common* is the ability of people to live together well in a community, the power of plurality: recognizing that conflicts are inherent to institutional life, are open and negotiable, and can lead to new ways of living together. It's within this sense of power-in-common that our commitment and our ability to deliberate well is crucial – to recognize and respect others and work together to imagine what new forms of life or organization might look like.

There have been a number of scholarly criticisms of Ricoeur's work that may be read at leisure. I'd like to end this chapter by looking at how we can take his work into the context of managing organizations. How it might offer a different lens on ethical management. Ricoeur places ethics as a moral and relational activity, around the fundamental challenge to *live well with others in just institutions*. This seems like an ideal we can extend to our organizational lives. In doing so, it's important to have ethical codes of conduct because they establish the moral norms against which we can evaluate ethical action. But what is crucially important to ethical organizational practice, to managing organizations in ethical ways, is the ethical intention and action of individual organizational members. Ethics is about *who we are and how we relate to others*, and this becomes particularly important in asymmetrical relationships – where one person has power over another. This means figuring out who I am as a person and as a manager, recognizing that I am responsible for what I do and say, while also being responsible for others. In fact, I cannot separate myself from others,

in both a particular and a general sense. This means being self reflexive, questioning my assumptions and actions, and being critically
reflexive about organizational policies and practices so that I do not,
in Ricoeur's terms, do violence to others. I began this chapter by saying that I'm a moral optimist – I think it's a prerequisite to living your life
in this way. As Chris Grey says at the end of the very first *Very Short* ...
book 'The stakes are very high. What kind of a world do you want?'

and so ...?

So let's assume we want to manage ethically – and by this I mean in
responsive and responsible ways – what might we do? Well, we need
to begin by recognizing that we are no longer well served by some
forms of current management and organizational practices; that there
are possibilities for new forms of ethical practice that we can successfully
negotiate with organizational members; and that central to this is my
own sense of who I am and how I relate to others.

I want to give the last word to one of my students, who really captured
in a very practical way the implications of Ricoeur's ideas on ethical
selfhood for managers. He ended his paper by saying:[8]

> First, I want to work more closely with other effective leaders who apply
> reflexive or highly ethical approaches to their work (e.g. Duffy Swan or
> Don Chalmers). Often these types of leaders operate quietly but effec-
> tively and I will need to search for them in unexpected places. As I
> learned from a classmate, Don Chalmers quietly volunteers his time at
> the Road Runner Food Bank. I plan to spend more of my time provid-
> ing volunteer services now too. Rich Marquez listed many attributes
> of successful leaders. I hope to focus more on those attributes I am
> weakest in such as humility for self and empathy with others. I also
> intend to search for non-traditional leaders such as those who provide
> services to me and my organization. I know I often overlook the quiet
> leadership exhibited by those who work in service roles. In my per-
> sonal life my wife often serves as my coach and mentor in being a parent
> leader for my children. I plan to seek her help more in better under-
> standing adult leadership issues, especially gender issues.
> Second, I am personally committed to reading and learning more
> about the philosophies of leadership espoused by Chatterjee (1998)
> and other 'non-traditional' or western leadership writers. My exposure

to and understanding of leadership philosophies in other cultures is too limited. I work with others from different cultures and I hope to better understand and appreciate our mutual values and differences. I am seriously considering taking educational classes in meditation and eastern philosophies and participating in cultural events to help me to better understand and apply cultural norms that differ from my own.

Finally, the most important element of my personal growth plan will be my ability to encourage an enduring generative learning approach to life and a critically reflexive view of my own actions. Finding a mentor may be especially helpful for achieving this goal. As Sheri Milone pointed out, developing a relationship with a mentor can be most beneficial for becoming a more aware and effective leader. I will need to search for such a mentor as there are many effective leaders in my organization. However I do not expect to easily find someone with the skills and philosophies I hope to nourish. Until I am successful at finding such a willing mentor I intend to develop a personal mental checklist or mindset that operates intuitively to help me be a more reflexive thinker. I also intend to develop a feedback or performance monitoring behavior (Drucker, 1999) that warns me when I have strayed. However, I must rely for now on my own mental discipline to develop and stay true to this leadership growth strategy. It will be a challenge but I expect to meet it. I will be an effective Philosopher Leader!

notes

1   See http://unpan1.un.org/intradoc/groups/public/documents/UN/UNPAN001963.pdf for information on the 10th International Anti-Corruption Conference (2001).
2   http://www.time.com/time/magazine/article/0,9171,1001826-2,00.html (accessed 30.7.2008).
3   See Armenakis (2002) for an interview with Morton-Thiokol Engineer Roger Boisjoly on ethics.
4   http://www.benjerry.com (accessed 2.12.2006).
5   Based on a personal communication from Normi Noel (1995).
6   See, for example, Husserl, 1983.
7   http://www.webcastr.com/videos/politics/edwards-webisode-1-plane-truths.html (accessed 14/8/2008).
8   Quoted with permission.

Conclusion…

In writing the conclusion to the book, I ended up with a long version and a short version – a bit like writing two different endings to a story. The long version summarized and explained the key themes, based on the golden rule of 'Telling the reader what you said'. But we've dealt with some challenging ideas about management and I wanted to capture the nub. The short version (the one here) is the pithy story, which, if you've already read the book will mean you'll look at the key issues and hopefully say 'yep', 'got that', 'makes sense', and 'at last, it all falls into place!'…

And if you are one of those people who like to know the ending before you read the story, then these snippets will hopefully intrigue you enough to want to read more.

So here goes:

This is a book offering a different way of thinking about management – it's not a book about management techniques.

Management and managers are important in today's world because what they do has an impact on everyone's lives.

Despite 100 years of management theories and techniques, managing is still a difficult and fraught process – most of us have experienced working for ineffective managers, or had a bad experience as a customer.

Why is managing so difficult? Because managers are like the rest of us – human and fallible.

And because people are not the coherent and malleable cluster of well-defined characteristics, fixed intentions and predictable actions that conventional management theories assume. Whatever and wherever managers manage, they can't avoid communicating with people.

People interpret the world and themselves differently; we have our own ideas about what's important and what needs to be done, and we like to do things our own way. We are naturally inquisitive, suspicious, we love, laugh, get scared, and dislike others. This doesn't stop the moment we walk into work. And what's rational to me is not necessarily rational to you – why should I buy into your version of rationality?

So life in organizations is messy, complex, open to various interpretations and therefore contestable – it's not predictable and controllable.

This surely means that the more ways managers have of viewing the world and of exploring possibilities, the better able they will be to manage in responsive, responsible and ethical ways.

So what if we question taken-for-granted views about management, and explore some different ways of thinking about management and managers?

Managing is about somehow connecting with people, recognizing and respecting differences, and creating meaning. Managing is relational and reflexive.

This means that instead of taking a realist view of the world as existing outside us, we assume that we have a dialectical relationship with our social world – we shape and are shaped by our experience as we talk and interact with others. We socially construct our world.

Language is therefore important, because we shape meaning, understanding and actions in relationally responsive interactions and conversations with others. But language is not precise – it works in subtle ways. We need to be aware of how our conversations might work.

We can use these ideas about language to both *understand* and *do* management differently. So what might we see if we look at organization culture, power and responsibility within relationships of difference and language? How might this influence the way we manage people and organizations? Can managers become cultural explorers and adventurers rather than manipulators?

Managing relationally is about dialogue not monologue, seeing conversations as crucial ways of figuring out between us what needs to be done.

And managers should be ethical – but we are still rocked by corporate scandals. Why? Does it have something to do with the focus on efficiency and on management techniques as value-neutral activities?

What if ethical management is both relational *and* institutional? About how we treat people and live our lives with others as well as moral codes of practice?

Being ethical means understanding who we are in relation to others, and recognizing that we have a moral and social responsibility to understand what we can and should expect of ourselves and others.

Being a manager is inseparable from who we are and how we relate to others, which means being *care*-ful and thoughtful in what we say and do.

Which brings us back to managing as relational and reflexive...

References

Acker, J. (2005) *Class Questions: Feminist Answers*. Roman Altamira Press.

Adams, G.P. (1911) 'Beyond moral idealism', *Harvard Theological Review*, 4 (2): 229–40.

Agar, M. (1994) *Language Shock: Understanding the Culture of Conversation*. New York, NY: Perennial.

Alvesson, M. and Deetz, S. (2000) *Doing Critical Management Research*. London: Sage.

Alvesson, M. and Willmott, H. (eds) (1992) *Critical Management Studies*. London: Sage.

Alvesson, M. and Willmott, H. (1996) *Making Sense of Management: A Critical Introduction*. London: Sage.

Argyris, C. (1982) *Reasoning, Learning and Action: Individual and Organizational*. San Francisco: Jossey-Bass.

Argyris, C. (1991) 'Teaching smart people how to learn', *Harvard Business Review*, 69 (3): 99–110.

Argyris, C. and Schön, D. (1974) *Theory in Practice: Increasing Professional Effectiveness*. San Francisco: Jossey-Bass.

Armenakis, A.A. (2002) Boisjoly on ethics: an interview with Roger Boisjoly, *Journal of Management Inquiry*, 11 (3): 274–81.

Ashcraft, K.L. (2001a) 'Organized dissonance: feminist bureaucracy as hybrid form', *Academy of Management Journal*, 44 (6): 1301–22.

Ashcraft, K.L. (2001b) 'Feminist organizing and the construction of "alternative" community', in J.G. Shepherd and E.W. Rothenbuhler (eds), *Communication and Community*. Mahwah, NJ: LEA Publishers. pp. 79–110.

Ashcraft, K.L. and Mumby, D. (2004) *Reworking Gender: A Feminist Communicology of Organization*. Thousand Oaks, CA: Sage.

Austin, J.L. (1962) *How to Do Things with Words*. Cambridge, MA: Harvard University Press.

Bakhtin, M.M. (1981) *The Dialogical Imagination: Four Essays by M.M. Bakhtin,* edited by M. Holquist, trans. C. Emerson and M. Holquist. Austin: University of Texas Press [reprinted 2002].

Bakhtin, M.M. (1984) *Problems of Dostoevsky's Poetics*, Manchester: Manchester University Press.

Bakhtin, M.M. (1986) *Speech Genres and Other Late Essays*, trans. V.W. McGee. Austin: University of Texas Press [reprinted 1996].

Barnard, C. (1938) *The Functions of the Executive*. Cambridge, MA: Harvard University Press.

Baudrillard, J. (1994) *Simulacra and Simulations*, trans. S.F. Glaser. Ann Arbor: University of Michigan Press.

Bentham, J. (1789) *An Introduction to the Principles of Morals and Legislation.*

Berger, P.L. and Luckmann, T. (1966) *The Social Construction of Reality: A Treatise in the Sociology of Knowledge*. New York: Anchor Books, Doubleday.

Bhabha, H.K. (1994) *The Location of Culture*. London: Routledge.

Boje, D.M. (1991) 'The storytelling organization: a study of story performance in an office-supply firm', *Administrative Science Quarterly*, 36 (1): 106–26.

Boje, D.M. (1994) 'Organizational storytelling. The struggles of pre-modern, modern and postmodern organizational learning discourses', *Management Learning*, 25 (3): 433–61.

Boje, D.M. (1995) 'Stories of the storytelling organization: a postmodern analysis of Disney as Tamara-land', *Academy of Management Journal*, 38 (4): 997–1035.

Boje, D.M. and Rosile, G.A. (1997) Restorying reengineering: some deconstructions and postmodern alternatives, *Communication Research*, 24 (6): 631–69.

Borofsky, R. (2005) *Yanomami: The Fierce Controversy and What We Can Learn from It*. Berkeley: University of California Press.

Boyatzis, R.E. (1982) *The Competent Manager: A Model for Effective Performance*. New York: John Wiley & Sons.

Brewis, J. (1999) 'How does it feel? Women managers, embodiment and changing public sector cultures', in S. Whitehead and R. Moodley (eds), *Transforming Managers: Gendering Change in the Public Sector*. London: UCL Press.

Brown, A.D. and Humphreys, M. (2006) 'Organizational identity and place: a discursive exploration of hegemony and resistance', *Journal of Management Studies*, 43 (2): 231–57.

Butler, J. (1990) *Gender Trouble: Feminism and the Subversion of Identity*. New York: Routledge [reprinted 1999].

Butler, J. (1993) *Bodies That Matter: On the Discursive Limits of Sex*. London: Routledge.

Calas, M. and Smircich, L. (1992) 'Using the "F" word: feminist theories and the social consequences of organizational research', in A.J. Mills and P. Tancred (eds), *Gendering Organizational Analysis*. Newbury Park, CA: Sage.

Carlson, S. (1951) *Executive Behaviour*. Stockholm: Strömbergs.

Chatterjee, D. (1998) *Leading Consciously: A Pilgrimage Toward Self-Mastery*. Boston: Butterworth-Heinemann.

Chia, R. and Morgan, S. (1996) 'Educating the philosopher manager: de-signing the times', *Management Learning*, 27 (1): 37–64.

Clifford, J. (1983) 'On ethnographic authority', *Representations*, 1 (2): 118–46.

Collinson, D. (1992) *Managing the Shopfloor: Subjectivity, Masculinity and Workplace Culture*. Berlin: De Gruyter.

Cunliffe, A.L. (2001) 'Managers as practical authors: reconstructing our understanding of management practice', *Journal of Management Studies*, 38 (3): 351–71.

Cunliffe, A.L. (2002a) 'Social poetics: a dialogical approach to management inquiry', *Journal of Management Inquiry*, 11 (2): 128–46.

Cunliffe, A.L. (2002b) 'Reflexive dialogical practice in management learning', *Management Learning*, 33 (1): 35–61.

Cunliffe, A.L. (2008) 'Orientations to social constructionism: relationally-responsive social constructionism and its implications for knowledge and learning', *Management Learning*, 39 (2): 123–39.

Cunliffe, A.L. (2009) 'The philosopher leader: on relationalism, ethics and reflexivity – a critical perspective on teaching leadership', *Management Learning*, 40 (1): 87–101.

Deetz, S.A. (1992) *Democracy in an Age of Corporate Colonization: Developments in Communication and the Politics of Everyday Life*. Albany: State University of New York Press.

Deetz, S.A., Tracy, S.J. and Simpson, J.L. (2000) *Leading Organizations Through Transition*. Thousand Oaks, CA: Sage.

Derrida, J. (1978) *Writing and Différance*. London: Routledge & Kegan Paul.

Dewey, J. (1910) *How We Think*. Mineola, NY: Dover Publications, Inc. [reprinted 1997].

Drucker, P.F. (1973) *Management: Tasks, Responsibilities, Practices*. New York: Harper & Row.

Drucker, P. (1999) 'Managing oneself', *Harvard Business Review*, 77 (2): 65–74.

Eisenhardt, K. (1989) 'Agency theory: an assessment and review', *Academy of Management Review*, 14 (1): 57–74.

Eisenstein, H. (1996) *Inside Agitators: Australian Femocrats and the State*. Philadelphia, PA: Temple University Press.

EOWA (2006) *Australian Census of Women in Leadership*. (www.eowa. gov.au/Australian_Women_in_Leadership_Census/2006/2006.asp).

Fairclough, N. (1992) *Discourse and Social Change*. Cambridge, MA: Polity Press.

Fairclough, N. (2003) *Analyzing Discourse: Textual Analysis for Social Research*. London: Routledge.

Fairhurst, G. (2007) *Discursive Leadership: In Conversation with Leadership Psychology*. Thousand Oaks, CA: Sage.

Fairhurst, G. and Sarr, R. (1996) *The Art of Framing*. San Francisco: Jossey-Bass.

Fayol, H. (1949) *General and Industrial Management*. London: Pitman [first published in 1916].

Fletcher, J. (1998) 'Relational practice: a feminist reconstruction of work', *Journal of Management Inquiry*, 7 (2): 163–88.

Follett, M.P. (1918) *The New State: Group Organization and the Solution of Popular Government*. New York: Longman, Green & Co.

Follett, M. P. (1924) *Creative Experience*. New York: Longman, Green & Co.

Ford, J. (2006) 'Discourses of leadership: gender, identity and contradiction in a UK public sector organization', *Leadership*, 2 (1): 77–99.

Ford, J. and Harding, N. (2007) 'Move over management: we are all leaders now', *Management Learning*, 38 (5): 1350–76.

Ford, J.D., Ford, L.W. and McNamara, R.T. (2002) 'Resistance and the background conversations of change', *Journal of Organizational Change Management*, 15 (2): 105–21.

Foucault, M. (1970) *The Order of Things. An Archaeology of the Human Sciences*. London: Routledge.

Foucault, M. (1972) *The Archaeology of Knowledge*, trans. by A.M. Sheridan Smith. New York: Pantheon Books.

Foucault, M. (1980) *The History of Sexuality, Vol. 1, An Introduction*. New York: Vintage Books.

Foucault, M. (1988) *The Care of the Self: The History of Sexuality*. New York: Vintage Books.

French, R. and Grey, C. (eds) (1996) *Rethinking Management Education*. Sage: London.

Gabriel, Y. (1995) 'The unmanaged organization: stories, fantasies and subjectivity', *Organization Studies*, 16 (3): 477–501.

Gagliardi, P. (ed.) (1990) *Symbols and Artifacts: Views of the Corporate Landscape*. Berlin and New York: de Gruyter.

Gagliardi, P. (1999) 'Exploring the aesthetic side of organizational life', in S.R. Clegg, and C. Hardy (eds), *Studying Organization: Theory and Method*. London: Sage.

Garfinkel, H. (1967) *Studies in Ethnomethodology*. Englewood Cliffs, NJ: Prentice-Hall.

Geertz, C. (1983) *Local Knowledge*. New York: Basic Books.

Gherardi, S. (1995) *Gender, Symbolism and Organizational Cultures*. London: Sage.

Ghoshal, S. (2005) 'Bad management theories are destroying good management practices', *Academy of Management Learning and Education*, 4 (1): 75–91.

Gilligan, C. (1982) *In a Different Voice: Psychological Theory and Women's Development*. Cambridge, MA: Harvard University Press.

Gilligan, C. (1995) 'Hearing the difference: theorizing connection', *Hypatia*, 10 (2): 120–27.

Goffman, E. (1959) *The Presentation of Self in Everyday life*. London: Allen Lane.

Goffman, E. (1961) *Asylums*. Harmondsworth: Penguin [reprinted 1976].

Goffman, E. (1967) *Interaction Ritual: Essays on Face-to-face Behavior*. New York: Random House Inc.

Gowler, D. and Legge, K. (1996) 'The meaning of management and the management of meaning', in S. Linstead, R. Grafton Small and P. Jeffcutt (eds), *Understanding Management*. London: Sage. pp. 34–50.

Gramsci, A. (1971) *Selections from the Prison Notebooks*, Trans. Q. Hoare and G. Nowell-Smith. New York: International.

Greener, I. (2007) 'The politics of gender in the NHS: impression management and "getting things done"', *Gender, Work and Organization*, 14 (3): 281–99.

Grey, C. (2008) *A Very Short, Fairly Interesting and Reasonably Cheap Book About Studying Organizations*. London: Sage.

Grey, C. and Willmott, H. (eds) (2005) *Critical Management Studies: A Reader*. Oxford: Oxford University Press.

Gulick, L. and Urwick, L. (eds) (1937) *Papers on the Science of Administration*. New York: Institute of Public Administration.

Hales, C.P. (1986) 'What do managers do? A critical review', *Journal of Management Studies*, 23 (1): 88–115.

Harding, N. (2002) 'On the manager's body as an aesthetics of control', *Tamara: Journal of Critical Postmodern Organization Science*, 2 (1): 63–76.

Harding, N. (2003) *The Social Construction of Management: Texts and Identities*. London: Routledge.

Hatch, M.J. (1997) 'Irony and the social construction of contradiction in the humor of a management team', *Organization Science*, 8 (3): 275–88.

Hatch, M.J. and Cunliffe, A.L. (2006) *Organization Theory: Modern, Symbolic, and Postmodern Perspectives*. Oxford: Oxford University Press.

Heidegger, M. (1966) *Discourse on Thinking: A Translation of Gelassenheit*, trans. J.M. Anderson and E. Hans Freund. New York: Harper & Row.

Hirigoyen, M.-F. (2005) *Stalking the Soul: Emotional Abuse and the Erosion of Identity*, trans. H. Marx and T. Moore. New York Helen Marx Books.

Hobbes, T. (1651) *Leviathan: The Matter, Forme and Power of a Commonwealth Ecclesiastical and Civil*.

Hochschild, A.R. (1983) *The Managed Heart: Commercialization of Human Feeling*. Berkeley: University of California Press.

Hodgson, D. (2005) 'Putting on a professional performance: performativity, subversion and project management', *Organization*, 12 (1): 51–68.

Hofstede, G. (1985) 'The interaction between national and organizational value systems', *Journal of Management Studies*, 22 (4): 347–57.

Hofstede, G. (2001) *Culture's Consequences: Comparing Values, Behaviors, Institutions and Organizations* (2nd edition). Thousand Oaks, CA: Sage.

Höpfl, H. (2002) 'Playing the part: reflections on aspects of mere performance in the customer–client relationship', *Journal of Management Studies*, 39 (2): 255–67.

Horne, J.H. and Lupton, T. (1965) 'The work activities of "middle managers" – an exploratory study', *Journal of Management Studies*, 2 (1): 14–33.

Husserl, E. (1983) *Ideas Pertaining to a Pure Phenomenology and to a Phenomenological Philosophy*. First Book (trans. F. Kersten). Netherlands: Kluwer Academic Publishers [reprinted 1998].

Jackall, R. (1988) *Moral Mazes: The World of Corporate Managers*. New York: Oxford University Press.

Kahney, L. (2008) 'How Apple got everything right by doing everything wrong', *Wired Magazine*. http://www.wired.com/techbiz/it/magazine/1604/bz_apple?currentPage=1 (accessed 28.8.08).

Kakabadse, A., Bank, J. and Vinnicombe, S. (2004) *Working in Organizations* (2nd edition). Aldershot: Gower Publishing.

Kant, I. (1785) *Fundamental Principles of the Metaphysic of Morals*.

Kepner, C.H. and Tregoe, B.B. (1965) *The Rational Manager: A Systematic Approach to Problem Solving and Decision-making*. New York: McGraw Hill.

Kohlberg, L. (1969) 'Stage and sequence: the cognitive-developmental approach to socialization', in D.A. Goslin (ed.), *Handbook of Socialization Theory and Research*. Chicago: Rand McNally. pp. 347–480.

Kotter, J.P. (1977) 'Power, dependence, and effective management', *Harvard Business Review*, 55 (4): 125–36.

Kotter, J.P. (1982) *The General Managers*. New York: Free Press.

Kunda, G. (1992) *Engineering Culture*. Philadelphia, PA: Temple University Press.

Laclau, E. and Mouffe, C. (1985) *Hegemony and Socialist Strategy: Towards a Radical Democratic Politics*. London: Verso.

Lawler, E.E. (ed.) (1985) *Doing Research That is Useful in Theory and Practice*. San Francisco: Jossey-Bass.

Learmonth, M. and Harding, N. (2006) 'Evidence-based management: the very idea', *Public Administration*, 84 (2): 245–66.

Linstead, S. (2006) 'The comedy of ethics: the New York four, the duty of care and organizational bystanding', in R. Westwood and C. Rhodes (eds), *Humour, Work and Organization*. London: Routledge. pp. 203–31.

Lukes, S. (1974) *Power: A Radical View*. London: Macmillan.

MacIntyre, A. (1981) *After Virtue: A Study in Moral Theory.* Notre Dame, IN: University of Notre Dame Press.

Management Learning (2009) Special Issue on 'Teaching from Critical Perspectives', 40 (1).

Marcus, G.E. and Fischer, M. (1986) *Anthropology as Cultural Critique.* Chicago: University of Chicago Press.

Marshall, J. (1995) 'Gender and management: a critical review of research', *British Journal of Management,* 6 (special issue): S53–S62.

Martin, J. (1990) 'Deconstructing organizational taboos: the suppression of gender conflict in organizations', *Organization Science,* 1 (4): 339–59.

Maslow, A.H. (1943) 'A theory of human motivation', *Psychological Review,* 50: 370–96.

Medvedev, P.N. and Bakhtin, M.M. (1978) *The Formal Method in Literary Scholarship: A Critical Introduction to Sociological Poetics,* trans A.J. Wehrle. Baltimore, MD: Johns Hopkins University Press.

Merleau-Ponty, M. (1962) *Phenomenology of Perception,* trans. by C. Smith. London and New York: Routledge [reprinted 2004].

Merleau-Ponty, M. (1964) *Signs,* trans. by R.C. McCleary. Evanston, IL: Northwestern University Press.

Mill, J.S. (1861) *Representative Government.*

Mintzberg, H. (1973) *The Nature of Managerial Work.* New York: Harper & Row.

Mirchandani, K. (2003) 'Challenging racial silences in studies of emotion work: contributions from anti-racist feminist theory', *Organization Studies,* 24 (5): 721–42.

Morgan, G. (1986) *Images of Organization.* London: Sage [reprinted 2006].

Organization Science (1998) Special Issue on 'Improvisation as a Metaphor for Organizing', 9 (5).

Orlikowski, W. and Hoffman, J.D. (1997) 'An improvisational model for change management: the case of Groupware Technologies', *Sloan Management Review,* 38 (2): 11–21.

Palmer, I. and Hardy, C. (2000) *Thinking About Management: Implications of Organizational Debates for Practice.* London: Sage.

Parker, M. (ed.) (1998) *Ethics and Organizations.* London: Sage.

Parker, M. (2002) *Against Management: Organization in the Age of Materialism.* Cambridge: Polity Press.

Peters, T.J. and Waterman, R.H. (1982) *In Search of Excellence: Lessons from America's Best Run Companies.* New York: Harper & Row.

Pfeffer, J. (1992) *Managing with Power.* Boston: Harvard Business School Press.

Pfeffer, J. and Fong, C.T. (2002) 'The end of business schools? Less success than meets the eye', *Academy of Management Learning and Education,* 1 (1): 78–95.

Pfeffer, J. and Sutton, R.I. (2006) 'Evidence-based management', *Harvard Business Review*, 84 (1): 62–74.

Prasad, A. and Prasad, P. (2001) '(Un)willing to resist? The discursive production of local workplace opposition', *Studies in Culture, Organizations and Societies*, 7 (1): 105–25.

Pullen, A. (2006) *Managing Identity*. Basingstoke: Palgrave Macmillan.

Rawls, J. (1971) *A Theory of Justice*. Cambridge, MA: Belknap Press of Harvard University Press.

Rice, J.H. (1960) 'Existentialism for the businessman', *Harvard Business Review*, 38 (2): 135–43.

Ricoeur, P. (1992) *Oneself as Another*, trans. K. Blamey. Chicago: University of Chicago Press.

Ritzer, G. (1995) *The McDonaldization of Society: An Investigation into the Changing Character of Contemporary Social Life*. Thousand Oaks, CA: Pine Forge Press.

Said, E.W. (1993) *Culture and Imperialism*. New York: Knopf.

Salancik, G.R. and Pfeffer, J. (1977). 'Who gets power – and how they hold on to it: a strategic contingency model of power', *Organizational Dynamics*, 5 (3): 3–21.

Sartre, J.-P. (1956) *Being and Nothingness: A Phenomenological Essay on Ontology*. New York: Citadel Press, Kensington Publishing. [reprinted 2001].

Sartre, J.-P. (1965) *Essays in Existentialism*. New York: Citadel Press, Kensington Publishing [reprinted 1993].

Saussure, F. de (1959 [1911]) *Course in General Linguistics*, trans. Wade Baskin. New York: McGraw-Hill.

Sayles, L.R. (1964) *Managerial Behavior*. New York: McGraw-Hill.

Schein, E.H. (1985) *Organizational Culture and Leadership* (2nd edition). San Francisco: Jossey-Bass.

Schön, D.A. (1983) *The Reflective Practitioner: How Professionals Think in Action*. New York: Basic Books.

Schultz, M., Hatch, M.J. and Larsen, M.H. (2002) *The Expressive Organization: Linking Identity, Reputation and the Corporate Brand*. Oxford: Oxford University Press.

Sex and Power 2008. Equality and Human Rights Commission. http://www.equalityhumanrights.com (accessed 30.10.08).

Shotter, J. (1992) 'Social constructionism and realism: adequacy or accuracy?' *Theory and Psychology*, 2 (2): 175–82.

Shotter, J. (1993) *Conversational Realities: Constructing Life through Language*. London: Sage.

Shotter, J. and Cunliffe, A.L. (2002) 'Managers as practical authors: everyday conversations for action', in D. Holman and R. Thorpe (eds), *Management and Language: The Manager as Practical Author*. London: Sage. pp. 15–37.

Simon, H. (1955) 'A behavioral model of rational choice', *Quarterly Journal of Economics*, 69: 99–118.

Sims, D. (2003) 'Between the millstones: a narrative account of the vulnerability of middle managers' storytelling', *Human Relations*, 56 (10): 1195–211.

Stewart, R. (1967) *Managers and Their Jobs* . Maidenhead: McGraw-Hill

Stewart, R. (1976) *Contrasts in Management*. Maidenhead: McGraw-Hill.

Stewart, R. (1982) *Choices for the Manager.* Englewood Cliffs, NJ: Prentice-Hall.

Strati, A. (1999) *Organization and Aesthetics*. London: Sage.

Sveningsson, S. and Alvesson, M. (2003) 'Managing managerial identities: organizational fragmentation, discourse and identity struggle', *Human Relations*, 56 (10): 1163–93.

Tannen, D. (1995) *Gender and Discourse*. Oxford: Oxford University Press.

Tannen, D. (2001) *Talking from 9 to 5: Women and Men at Work*. New York: Harper Collins Paperbacks.

Taylor, C. (2004) *Modern Social Imaginaries*. Durham, NC: Duke University Press.

Taylor, F.W. (1911) *The Principles of Scientific Management*. New York: Harper & Row.

Thadhani, R. (2005) 'Between monocles and veils: glimpses in postcolonial public administration', *International Journal of Public Administration*, 28 (11/12): 973–88.

Thomas, R. and Linstead, A. (2002) 'Losing the plot? Middle managers and identity', *Organization*, 9 (1): 71–93.

Vaill, P.B. (1989) *Managing as a Performing Art: New Ideas for a World of Chaotic Change*. San Francisco: Jossey-Bass.

Vera, D. and Crossan, M. (2004) 'Theatrical improvisation: lessons for organizations', *Organization Studies*, 25 (5): 727–49.

Watson, T.J. (2001) *In Search of Management: Culture, Chaos and Control in Managerial Work*. London: Routledge.

Watson, T.J. and Harris, P. (1999) *The Emergent Manager*. London: Sage.

Weber, M. (1947) *The Theory of Social and Economic Organization* (ed. A.H. Henderson and T. Parsons). Glencoe, IL: Free Press [first published in 1924].

Weick, K.E. (1995) *Sensemaking in Organizations*. London: Sage.

Weick, K.E. (1998) 'Improvisation as a mindset for organizational analysis', *Organization Science*, 9 (5): 543–55.

Weick, K.E. (2001) *Making Sense of the Organization*. Oxford: Blackwell Publishers.

Welsh, M.A. and Dehler, G.E. (2007) 'Whither the MBA? Or the withering of MBAs?' *Management Learning*, 38 (4): 405–23.

Whetton, D.A. and Cameron, K.S. (1983) 'Management skill training: a needed addition to the management curriculum', *Exchange: The Organizational Behavior Teaching Journal*, 8 (2): 10–15.

Willmott, H. (1994) 'Management education: provocations to a debate', *Management Learning*, 25 (1): 105–36.

Willmott, H. (1998) 'Towards a new ethics? The contributions of post-structuralism and posthumanism', in M. Parker (ed.), *Ethics and Organizations*. London: Sage. pp. 76–121.

Zukin, S. (1996) *The Cultures of Cities*. Malden, MA: Blackwell Publishers.

additional reading

Alvesson, M. (1994) 'Talking in organizations: managing identity and impressions in an advertising agency', *Organization Studies*, 15 (4): 535–63.

Alvesson, M. and Karreman, D. (2000) 'Varieties of discourse: on the study of organizations through discourse analysis', *Human Relations*, 53 (9): 1125–49.

Barrett, F.J., Thomas, G.F. and Hocevar, S.P. (1995) 'The central role of discourse in large-scale change', *Journal of Applied Behavioral Science*, 31 (3): 352–73.

Clegg, S., Pitsis, T. and Kornberger, M. (2008) *Managing and Organizations: An Introduction to Theory and Practice*. London: Sage.

Collinson, D. and Hearn, M. (1997) (eds) *Men as Managers, Managers as Men: Critical Perspectives on Men, Masculinities and Management*. London: Sage.

Cooper, R. (1989) 'Modernism, postmodernism and organizational analysis 3: The contribution of Jacques Derrida', *Organization Studies*, 10 (4): 479–502.

Cunliffe, A.L. (2004) 'On becoming a critically reflexive practitioner', *Journal of Management Education*, 28 (4): 407–26.

Cunliffe, A.L. and Jun, J. (2005) 'The need for reflexivity in public administration', *Administration and Society*, 37: 225–42.

Donaldson, L. (2008) 'Ethics problems and problems with ethics: toward a pro-management theory', *Journal of Business Ethics*, 78 (3): 299–311.

Foucault, M. (1977) *Discipline and Punish: The Birth of the Prison*. London: Penguin.

Fournier, V. and Keleman, M. (2001) 'The crafting of community: recoupling discourses of management and womanhood', *Gender, Work and Organization*, 8 (3): 267–90.

Grey, C. (1996) 'Towards a critique of managerialism: the contribution of Simon Weil', *Journal of Management Studies*, 33 (5): 591–611.

Heidegger, M. (1978) *Basic Writings*, ed. by D.F. Krell. London: Routledge.

Holt, R. (2006) 'Principles and practice: rhetoric and the moral character of managers', *Human Relations*, 59 (12): 1659–80.

Jackson, B. (1996) 'Re-engineering the sense of self: the manager and the management guru', *Journal of Management Studies*, 33 (5): 571–90.

Kärreman, D. (2001) 'The scripted organization: dramaturgy from Burke to Baudrillard', in R. Westwood and S. Linstead (eds), *The Language of Organization*. London: Sage. pp. 89–111.

Manning, P.K. (2008) 'Goffman on organizations', *Organization Studies*, 29 (5): 677–99.

Mumby, D. (1998) 'Organizing men: power, discourse and the social construction of masculinity(s) in the workplace', *Communication Theory*, 8 (2): 164–83.

Prasad, A. (ed.) (2003) *Postcolonial Theory and Organization Analysis: A Critical Engagement*. New York: Palgrave Macmillan.

Quinn, R.E., Faerman, S.R., Thompson, M.P. and McGrath, M.R. (1990) *Becoming a Master Manager: A Competency Framework*. New York: Wiley.

Revans, R. (1971) *Developing Effective Managers: A New Approach to Business Education*. New York: Praeger.

Rowlinson, M., Toms, S. and Wilson, J.F. (2007) 'Competing perspectives on the "managerial revolution": from "managerialist" to "anti-managerialist"', *Business History*, 49 (4): 464–82.

Stewart, R., Smith, P., Blake, J. and Wingate, P. (1980) *The District Administrator in the National Health Service*. London: Pitman.

Tracy, S.J. (2000) 'Becoming a character for commerce: emotion labor, self-subordination, and discursive construction of identity in a total institution', *Management Communication Quarterly*, 14 (1): 90–128.

Index